The Ghost Tour of Great Britain
Derbyshire

The Ghost Tour
of Great Britain
Derbyshire

with *Most Haunted's* **Richard Felix**

breedon **books**
PUBLISHING

First published in Great Britain in 2005 by

The Breedon Books Publishing Company Limited

Breedon House, 3 The Parker Centre, Derby, DE21 4SZ.

ISBN 1 85983 478 7

Printed and bound by CPI Group, Bath Press, Bath, Avon.

CONTENTS

ACKNOWLEDGEMENTS

The production of this book would not have been possible
without the help and expertise of:

the other members of the Ghost Tour team,

Steve Lilley and Delicia Redfern

Jim Fearn

and all the staff at Breedon Books in Derby

LANDS
END
2003

NEW YORK 3147   JOHN O'GROATS 874

ISLES OF SCILLY 28   NATIONAL GHOST
LONGSHIPS LIGHTHOUSE 1½   TOUR

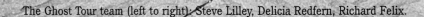

The Ghost Tour team (left to right): Steve Lilley, Delicia Redfern, Richard Felix.

PREFACE

When local historian Richard Felix opened a Heritage Centre in his home city of Derby, England, in 1992, even his far-reaching powers of perception could not have forecast how important a step he had taken.

The Heritage Centre, based in an area of the city known as St Peter's Churchyard, became the starting point for Richard's innovative ghost walks and within 12 years more than 150,000 people — many of them so fascinated by the concept that they visited from America — had booked in to be scared out of their wits.

Soon the Derby ghost walks took on legendary status and were attended by scores of would-be ghost hunters. The story unfolds as ghost walkers leave the Heritage Centre and are told that they are walking over the bodies of many of the victims of the Black Death. They head down St Peter's Street towards the site of Derby's first gaol, a place of incarceration for witches, heretics and traitors. The Lock-Up Yard, the scene of the brutal murder of a policeman, is visited next. A moment's reprieve permits the ghost-hunters to partake of another kind of spirit in the Tiger Bar, in preparation for a subterranean trip down into the barrel-vaulted tunnels beneath Derby's Guildhall. The story continues as the party heads across the Market Place, then on to the Cathedral, the Shire Hall (the scene of a horrendous pressing to death in 1665), before returning to the Heritage Centre for a Ghost Hunter's Supper — for those who can stomach the feast that is!

With the success of his ghost tours in Derby it became clear to Richard Felix that a formula that worked so well in one place would probably succeed in other towns and cities across the British Isles, and so when he was approached by film producer Stephen Lilley to record a remarkable DVD series – *The Ghost Tour of Great Britain* – he jumped at the chance. It was a mammoth, time-consuming task that relied on the great British public taking the idea seriously. And they did. The intrepid pair visited every major city and well over 40 counties throughout England, Scotland, Ireland and Wales and, with incredible attention to detail, they attempted to uncover explanations for each eerie haunting, researching library archives and interviewing credible witnesses, historians, renowned psychics and parapsychologists.

As interest in the ghost walks and *The Ghost Tour of Great Britain* increased, so did Richard Felix's fame as an authority on all things paranormal. He was invited to become the resident historical expert on the hugely popular Living TV show *Most Haunted*. Appropriately, one of the places investigated by *Most Haunted* was Derby Gaol – undoubtedly one of the most haunted sites in Britain. Situated in the basement of 50/51 Friar Gate, Derby Gaol is a working museum where visitors can see the actual cells where prisoners were kept. It was used as a prison from 1756 to 1828 and, following its acquisition by Richard Felix in 1997, has been restored to its original condition. Now visitors can try paranormal investigations using the latest hi-tech ghost-hunting equipment, just as the *Most Haunted* team did on film inside the Condemned Cell. Those of a fearless disposition can even sign up for a Derby Gaol Sleepover, comprising a mini ghost walk for an hour and a half around Friar Gate, a pie and porter supper and a bar that serves all night! A medium can also be arranged to carry out séances and private readings.

This book has been written to accompany the DVD series and recounts in words and pictures the chilling accounts of paranormal experiences uncovered by Richard Felix and Steve Lilley on their groundbreaking trip, *The Ghost Tour of Great Britain*.

PART ONE

GHOSTS

AND HOW

TO FIND

THEM

RICHARD'S THEORIES ABOUT GHOSTS

As I was raised in a haunted house, you will forgive me for having well-formed ideas about the existence of ghosts. After years of study and countless fascinating experiences, some of them truly frightening, I now consider myself an expert in the paranormal.

It may surprise you to learn, therefore, that as a child the very thought of spirits, ghouls and skeletons filled me with fear and dread. I was petrified by ghosts and, to a certain extent, I still am to this day. When I was no more than four years old I was locked into garages and garden sheds by so-called friends and told that the 'Green Ghost' was going to get me. Experiences such as this only served to fuel an already fertile imagination and as a child I would refuse to stay in any building on my own and would certainly never walk past a churchyard alone or even walk upstairs without someone's hand to hold. I spent many a night as a youngster lying wide awake beneath my bedclothes, waiting for a demonic being to stride into my bedroom, pull back the bedclothes and reveal its hideous face. Of course this never happened, but perhaps my way of facing up to my fears was to attempt to discover all I possibly could about how and why spirits haunt places.

In the early 1990s I started to conduct ghost walks around Derby – and 12 years later well over 150,000 people had been on a ghost tour of my home city. Derby's location, almost in the centre of the country, has underlined its great importance for almost 2,000 years and contributed to its prosperity. It has always been a crossing of the ways and was the scene of the last hanging, drawing and quartering to be carried out in England, the result of the last rebellion against the Crown to take place in this country.

However, every region of these isles has its own folklore and legends and in recognition of this Stephen Lilley and I embarked on *The Ghost Tour of Great Britain*. In less than three years we visited nearly every county in the land, looking for ghosts, talking to people who have seen ghosts and visiting haunted places. My experiences as an expert on the popular *Most Haunted* TV programme have broadened my horizons still further and put me in direct contact with the scariest places in Great Britain and beyond. Even today, however, I am still learning and remain grateful to the

folklorists and parapsychologists who continually surprise me with their thoughts and theories.

In this book, you will read chilling tales of hauntings, but I will also attempt to pass on, from my own experiences, the knowledge and details of the equipment you need to detect paranormal activity yourself. In short, everything you need to know to become a ghost-hunter.

First, however, you need to understand what a ghost is.

Some parapsychologists don't believe in life after death and put hauntings down to the influence of the living, not the dead. They attribute unexplained events to Extra Sensory Perception (ESP) – the psychic powers of living individuals who have the ability, for example, to move objects.

We are taught from an early age that we *can't* do certain things. If a door opens by itself, a spoon bends without any force being applied to it or a glass on a mantelpiece suddenly shatters, as adults we look for a logical explanation. Those who believe in ESP say that this desire to explain away inexplicable events is no more than a safety valve – far better to be a sceptic than attribute strange happenings to the power of the mind and run the risk of being ridiculed. And at least ESP and the idea of telepathic understanding between living creatures is a more comfortable theory to swallow than the spectre of the dead being trapped on earth as punishment for terrible crimes or through the tragedy and pain of an unexpected demise.

The idea of sharing our world – sometimes our own homes – with the spirits of dead people is uncomfortable to say the least, but I have met hundreds of sane, sober individuals who swear they have encountered a ghost. Intrigued? Well, before you read on, please make a note of the Richard Felix Rules of Ghost Hunting. First, you have to be an enthusiast. Second, you need to be a detective, and third, most certainly a sceptic. You have to explore all avenues when you look into a ghost's history and get to the bottom of the *reason* for the haunting.

For many, that would be enough. However, I passionately believe the ultimate aim of the ghost-hunter is to ask: 'How can I help?' If you're looking for nothing more than the cheap thrill of a scary experience, go and watch a horror movie. I feel that there's a responsibility attached to ghost-hunting. If an animal lover tracks down a caged gorilla, does he simply take a photograph of the sad ape and walk away? No, that's not enough – the final act has to be to release the creature from its pain. It is therefore important to understand that ghosts – whether the product of the living or the dead – haunt places for different reasons and I believe that there are at least five distinct types.

The dead returning

This is where a spirit is seeking some kind of 'closure', as our American friends might say. It can interact, is aware of its environment and knows you are there – it's a conscious entity that can even speak to you. To me, this is the most frightening type of ghost, but what's the reason for its existence? The basic premise is that while the spirit of a dead person remains on earth, the soul moves on to its eternal reward. So maybe our interactive ghosts have business on earth they haven't concluded or are somehow trapped and can't move on to where good souls go.

In the Middle Ages there was a strong belief in Purgatory – a state in between heaven and hell. Quite often human bones are found where ghosts have been seen for a number of years and a common theory is that troubled souls haunt the earth because they weren't buried properly. The way we depart this life isn't something most of us think too deeply about these days, but in bygone times people craved a decent burial. Could denial of the Last Rites or bitterness that their bones were interred in ground that was not consecrated create the energy of a troubled ghost, stubbornly waiting for a proper burial?

I spoke recently to a Cornish woman who told me that through the Church's influence in the Middle Ages and its warnings of eternal damnation, souls that had done bad deeds in life were simply too afraid to move on, so instead hovered on earth as ghosts.

This theory may help to explain why we don't see many modern ghosts – there was more fear in the past of the punishment for sins in death, hence the reluctance of some to take the step into the afterlife. Perhaps these days we are more relaxed about our wrong-doings and don't believe they have to be paid for when we die?

Some ghosts apparently don't have any choice about whether or not they move on to another place. We have long been told that individuals who have committed terrible crimes are condemned to walk this earth for eternity, repenting their sins. Marley's ghost in Charles Dickens's *A Christmas Carol* warns Scrooge to mend his ways, or face the prospect of dragging in death the heavy chains he has forged link by link throughout his corrupt life.

The fact that these interactive ghosts represent the dead returning and the spirits of real people – entities with intelligence – makes them difficult to track down. Why would a self-respecting ghost with the ability to interact allow itself to be nailed by a gang of hi-tech ghost-hunters wielding laser temperature readers?

The apparition

If you could take a camcorder and video player back in time 200 years, imagine how staggered the people of early 19th-century Britain would be at your ability to play back on a screen a particular event you had just recorded.

So why are we shocked today by the idea of a traumatic event, perhaps a terrible premature death, somehow recording itself naturally into rock, brickwork, or even soil? Stone in particular is an ideal recording medium because it contains silica, and it's my belief that the energy emanates out of the stone.

I believe electronic impulses emanate from the brain in the moments before death takes place, creating energy that imprints itself into the fabric of the location. When atmospheric conditions are right, the image created by this energy replays the scene. That's why you see an apparition as it was just before the person died, but it's no more real than watching John Wayne in an old cowboy movie. The Duke long ago rode off into the sunset to that big ranch in the sky – it's his image you see and hear on video and it's impossible for him to interact with you. The same can be said for apparitions.

The tragic scene is played out again and again, but this ghost can't interact – there's no sense of the apparition being aware of the living. Just like a favourite videotape that is played too often, apparitions tend to fade through time. There are stories of ghostly hauntings that have become less distinct down the years, starting out, for example, as a red lady in the 18th century, changing to a pink lady in the 19th century, then to a white lady in the 20th century before becoming no more than a pillar of light accompanied by the sound of footsteps.

Telepathic projection

Like the apparition, this ghost is created by a moment of crisis. We've all heard stories of the woman who sees the image of her husband stranded on a mountain or a soldier appearing to his family moments before he is killed in the trenches.

These are classic examples of the telepathic understanding between people who love each other. In some cases the person who appears as a 'ghost' doesn't actually die, because their appearance prompts a loved-one to summon help. We have all experienced that nagging voice in our head that tells us to visit a relative or friend we know is sick. It's a telepathic experience linked to high emotion.

Phantasm

This is a bizarre apparition that, some would say, proves that ghosts are as much to do with the living as the dead. In the 1888 Census of Hallucinations, a huge survey, the Society for Psychical Research interviewed people throughout the British Isles and Northern France and came up with a surprising statistic. It was discovered that where those questioned were actually able to identify the ghost they had seen, half of the 'ghosts' were still alive and in no danger at the time they were seen! Phantasms are created by another form of telepathy, where an individual, though alive, somehow places an image of himself elsewhere. Far-fetched? Well I have a first-hand account of a baker who, after he had retired, was seen by the new owner of the business as an apparition going about his duties in the bakery. The new owner assumed that he had seen a ghost and that the old baker must be dead. However, on further investigation he discovered that the old man was very much alive, but had little to do in retirement. Consequently he spent most of his time in solitude, daydreaming about his old job. In doing this he somehow provoked the ghostly image of himself to appear at his beloved bakery to be witnessed by the new owner.

Poltergeist

Poltergeists represent a big group of ghosts. There are two contrasting schools of thought on exactly what makes a poltergeist. The name comes from the mediaeval German words *polte* (noisy) and *geist* (ghost). Once again the definition of this ghost comes down to a battle between the living and the dead. One side of the argument believes poltergeists are mischievous, sometimes malevolent, spirits who inhabit a particular place, often a room. The other side goes with the theory of Recurrent Spontaneous Psycho Kinesis, or RSPK for short. They believe that living people, for reasons we don't understand, use the power of their own minds to affect their environments.

Scary movies have given many people a very definite idea of what poltergeists do. We have been drip-fed an image of mischievous spirits throwing objects across rooms, but poltergeist hauntings tend to be more measured than the cinematic interpretation suggests. More regularly they start with a scratching sound and then move on to the odd loud bang, progressing to unpleasant smells. Eventually objects start to move – not initially by floating across a room, but in an annoying way. A set of house keys you always leave on the kitchen table disappears, you hunt high and low and half an hour later you find them – exactly where you left them.

Then come phenomena known as 'small object displacement'. Everyday objects disappear from a room and reappear in a different place. The next stage of a poltergeist haunting is that unusual items appear from nowhere. Old wooden toys, teddy bears, and, at its most grisly, human bones, have all been reported as appearing in rooms. Eventually poltergeist activity progresses to the classic image of objects flying across a room. It's interesting to note though that objects in these reported cases are said to float in straight lines, rather than going up and down in an arc the way they would if you or I threw something in the air and let gravity take charge.

I have very seldom spoken to anyone who has been damaged physically or mentally by ghosts – nor have I heard of poltergeist activity resulting in objects actually hitting anyone. I believe poltergeist activity isn't either mischievous or malevolent, but a call for help. The longest poltergeist incidence I have encountered is a year, but more usually it's a matter of weeks or months.

Filming one episode of *Most Haunted*, our camera captured a teddy bear flying across a room where a child had died many years before.

It seems that poltergeists focus either on a particular person or on a particular place. I have spoken to parapsychologists who have totally sealed off a room where poltergeist activity had been reported. They left a camera running and there was absolutely no possible way the room could be interfered with by any living being. They waited outside and within a minute heard a huge smashing sound. Running into the room, they found the camera pointing at the floor and a teddy bear, last seen on a sofa, sitting with its paws up in front of the fire, as if to warm itself against the cold.

Quite often, poltergeist cases seem to have a living agent. It's normally people who are highly intelligent, creative and imaginative, possibly disturbed by family issues. It is claimed that emotionally charged individuals troubled, for example, by the onset of puberty, cause some poltergeist experiences. That is why it is so important to map out family relationships and areas where an individual might be emotionally charged before diving in with theories and solutions. Where poltergeist activity results from one person's emotional state, the issue needs to be treated with sensitivity and respect. Sometimes a far more sensible alternative to chasing the poltergeist is recommending sound medical assistance.

A GUIDE TO GHOST-HUNTING

If you regularly tune in to the *Most Haunted* TV show, you'll see us using all manner of sophisticated ghost-hunting equipment. There really are some superb ghost-hunting aids on the market these days, and I'd advise you to examine these hi-tech units if you are looking to back up investigation successes with scientific evidence.

However, when starting out as a ghost-hunter you can, if you wish, get away with pretty basic equipment, much of it to be found around the house.

A **torch** is essential and **candles** are useful too because in addition to giving soft light they can detect movements and draughts. Another 'must have' is a **tape recorder** or **Dictaphone**. A useful rule with regard to taping sound is not to leave your recorder running – it's painstaking and ultimately unrewarding to listen back to hours of tape after a ghost-hunting session. Much better to use your tape recorder only when you have asked your ghost a question – such as the classic 'Is anybody there?' Then switch on your recorder and leave it on for two or three minutes and you could get some very good results.

You can get away with an everyday **thermometer** to gauge sudden drops in temperature, but better still is a **laser thermometer**, which detects the temperature at exactly the point its red scan light hits and gives a reading on a handheld gauge.

Tape – such as household masking tape – is useful for taping off areas of activity or windows. A piece of **thread** can also be useful to section off small areas, such as a tabletop.

To assist in monitoring the movement of trigger objects, items that move during poltergeist activity, an upturned **transparent case** can come in handy. Try a plastic fish tank – and I'd recommend an empty one! Putting trigger objects underneath plastic makes for a more scientific examination of item movement because it eradicates the possibility of anything being moved by natural factors, such as draughts or wind.

In the absence of digital recording equipment, something as basic as a piece of **graph paper** at least gives you the opportunity to map out items on a table or in a room before and after a poltergeist haunting.

Dowsing rods are ghost-hunting implements you need to acquire a relationship with, and a feel for, quite literally! In simple terms the rods are two pieces of thin rigid wire, the consistency of a typical Firework Night sparkler and around 18 inches long in each case. Place each rod lightly between the first and second finger of each hand and, with fists clenched and facing away from the body, and elbows slightly bent, hold the rods out horizontally in front of you approximately six inches apart. Try them out in any space, particularly one where a haunting has been reported, and simply ask the rods to give you 'yes' and 'no' answers to questions. I believe you get a 'yes' when the rods cross inwards and a 'no' when they angle away from each other. If you ask if a spirit is in the room you are in and the answer is 'yes', you can then ask the rods to point in the direction of the spirit. Patience and concentration is needed, but in my experience dowsing rods really do work. I don't know *how* they work but my gut feeling is that it's something to do with the power of the mind transmitting itself through the body and into the rods. Ask me for a scientific explanation and I can offer none, but my own personal experience of using rods is both positive and genuine.

If and when you really catch the ghost-hunting bug you might want to invest in some of the incredibly sophisticated pieces of state-of-the-art equipment now on the market. Such is the interest that there are companies such as the British-based Spectral Electronics that now deal exclusively in ghost-hunting aids.

The **Electro-Magnetic Field (EMF) meter** has been used for several years now by ghost-hunters and by paranormal investigators. This hand-held machine, not much bigger than a TV remote control unit, can detect electro-magnetic presence in the fabric of buildings; useful when investigating, for example, regular reported sightings of an apparition in the same place. The latest generation of EMF meters, developed specifically for paranormal investigators, are ingenious because they filter out everyday electrical charges such as mains frequencies. With a pair of normal headphones you can also measure variations in electro-magnetic energies recorded by the meter.

The **Ultra-Sonic Unit** is pretty new on the market. In look and feel it is similar to an EMF meter with a display and an audio connection. Ultra-Sonic Units measure acoustic energies in ultrasound regions at frequencies of 20khz and above, a range of sound that bats and, significantly, dogs can hear, but way beyond normal human hearing. Animals generally seem more sensitive to paranormal activity than we humble humans and devices such as the Ultra-Sonic Unit help us to redress the balance. Previously some ghost-hunters would take dogs on investigations because they seemed to be able to pick up things that humans couldn't. With the head-phone connection you can monitor high-frequency sounds and, if you wish, record them onto your Dictaphone. Some of the more advanced paranormal investigation groups have even developed computer programs that enable users to store and interpret information using sounds recorded through Ultra-Sonic Units. These programs are available as free downloads on the Internet and can display spectrum analysis ranges that show, for example, energies recorded in different frequencies. So Ultra-Sonic Units do so much more than simply replicating the sensitivity of dogs, and the real beauty of them of course is you don't have to take them out for walks!

The **Negative-Ion Detector** is another 21st-century phenomenon. The low-light infrared filming we carry out on *Most Haunted* often shows up orbs, small objects that seem to fly through the air like tiny flying saucers. These orbs are believed to have some relation to high voltage or static electricity, a side effect of which is a surplus of negative ions. You can create your own electro-magnetic field through the old trick of rubbing a balloon against a jumper, creating an energy that allows the balloon to stick to a ceiling. This is the same type of energy picked up by Negative-Ion Detectors, which give out an audible beep to indicate activity.

Interviewing technique is also crucial, despite the availability of modern-day equipment that can make the business of ghost-hunting easier and ultimately more exciting. Investigators of paranormal activity must be prepared to talk to people who have witnessed a haunting when amassing evidence. It is essential therefore to develop an effective interviewing style. Devoting hour upon hour of your own time to ghost stakeouts is all very well, but it is always important to factor in the experiences of other people who have personal accounts to tell of activity in a particular case. It is rather like a detective cracking a criminal case: having first-hand evidence is fine, but to prove your case you need to accumulate witness statements. For these statements to be as effective as possible, like a police detective, you also need to develop a good interviewing technique. Let your subjects do the talking, prompt them with open-ended questions and gently but firmly ask them to stick to the facts of what they have personally seen or heard, not what they have been told by others.

Always record your interviews on a tape recorder or Dictaphone. Ask permission of your subject first of course, and respect their privacy, but recording interviews is important because it enables you to concentrate not only on what is being said, but on the *way* it is being said. Our intuition helps us form an impression of whether someone is speaking sincerely or lying through their teeth. Witnesses' body language will often either give them away or underline their credibility. If you are convinced by the sincerity of your witness the next step is to listen back to the tape and make a full transcript. This is where you, as a detective, must take a sceptical view of the evidence. If a particular witness informs you, for example, that a door in a particular building regularly slams shut for no reason, then look for a logical explanation. Is the activity caused by a through-draught that occurs naturally when another door is opened elsewhere in the house? If a witness reports the smell of tobacco in a particular room at certain times and attributes this to the presence of a pipe-smoking ghost, could it in fact be more to do with temperature changes inducing an odour in paintwork, plaster or old floorboards? Could the sound of ghostly footsteps be nothing more sinister than your neighbours in the house next door, movement in the rooms above or even thermostatically controlled central heating kicking in with a rumble and a thud?

In Tutbury Castle there's a 17th-century costume presented on a shop window-style mannequin that appears to sway entirely on its own. In fact the room where this costume is displayed shares the same old floorboards as the adjoining King's Bedroom at the Castle. Although a partition wall was erected to make one room into two at some stage in the Castle's history, the effect of walking in the King's Bedroom moves the floorboards in the adjoining room and sets the mannequin moving!

Your most reliable witnesses will inevitably be people who live or work in the place where they report paranormal activity. They will be aware of everyday sounds that have a natural cause and will be able to speak to you with greater authority about happenings that are genuinely unusual. The problem with ghost hunts and people whose experiences relate to a location they are not familiar with is that every small sound or movement seems to demand an explanation. It's far better to rely on the witness statements of people who are truly familiar with the place where a ghostly presence is reported. Give particular weight to the statements of those witnesses who stick to the facts of what they have experienced rather than speculating as to the cause. If they tell you they regularly hear footsteps in the cellar followed by a loud bang, but haven't any idea what causes this phenomenon, it's a more telling observation than someone who goes on to speculate that the activity is probably caused by the ghost of an unhappy monk who hanged himself in the

15th century, because Mrs Jones in the village reckons the house was once the site of a monastery…

A **methodical approach** is crucial for ghost-hunting. Sherlock Holmes may be a fictional detective, but he was given a very factual philosophy on detection. When approaching a case he would rule out the impossible and examine what he was left with, as this, he believed, was the truth, however improbable that truth seemed.

I can testify from personal experience to the emotion attached to seeing a ghost at first-hand and the careful analysis I went through afterwards to convince myself of what I had seen. It happened in Derby Gaol, not at dead of night during a low-light ghost hunt, but in the middle of the afternoon in a kitchen when I was on my mobile phone in conversation with a friend. Through the open door of the kitchen I saw a figure, the size of a person and grey as grey, move down one of the old gaol's corridors. Although there was no drop in temperature, I sensed it as well as seeing it. By the time I got to the actual door to the corridor, it had gone.

This experience frightened me, quite a lot. However, when I recovered I then went through the process of ruling out all the naturally occurring things that might have caused its appearance. Although what I saw had a misty appearance, it wasn't smoke, it wasn't steam and it wasn't the reflection of a car's headlights. There's a theory known as 'Standing Wave' that tells us that in certain conditions extractor fans in rooms, corridors and even in computers can give off an odd acoustic effect that creates the impression of something moving fleetingly at the very edge of an individual's vision and prompts terrible feelings of fear and anxiety. However, the grey mass I saw wasn't out of the corner of my eye; it was a full-on experience and I can think of no other explanation than my having witnessed a ghost.

Here is something strange but true: while filming an episode of *Most Haunted* I saw a spoon fly through the air. I wasn't the first person to the errant spoon when it landed and my slowness off the mark on this occasion probably saved me getting my fingers burned! In some instances items subject to poltergeist activity, whether cutlery, coffee cups or other general household objects, have been found to be red hot to the touch. This I put down to the poltergeist energy created in its movement, so approach with care!

Continuing the methodical approach to all things paranormal, it is important to log examples of poltergeist activity for future reference, so always weigh the object that has apparently moved and measure how far it has travelled. This statistical information can help you prove, for example, that items of a certain weight tend to travel a certain distance in a particular room. At the very least it is information you can pass on for others to quantify. Organisations such as the Society for Psychical Research will always be happy to offer assistance provided you have facts and figures to support your questions.

Original artefacts are always good for measuring powers of perception through a simple touching and sensing test. Anyone can try it, though some, inevitably, are more sensitive than others. Here's what you do, in a group if you wish: lay the palms of your hands lightly on an artefact – anything from a sideboard to a sword – and then clear your mind completely. Try to register signals from the item you are touching; then talk about it.

Folklore is the development of history rather than hard historical fact. For example, it may be factually correct that in the Middle Ages a woman leapt to her death from the north tower of a castle after her knight husband returned early from battle to discover her with a lover. The folklore element is the tale passed down through the ages that the apparition of a white lady is seen leaping from the same tower just before midnight, or that a candle will never burn when lit in the room at the top of the tower.

So how, as a ghost-hunter, do you try to bridge the gap between folklore and fact? First, as always, gain permission from the owners of the property you intend to investigate. You may even feel it is sensible to have a member of staff of the haunted building – a curator of the castle for example – present throughout the investigation. At the very least, draw up a written agreement with the owners or trustees of the building that your investigation has been sanctioned. I would then devise experiments suitable to the environment and probably arrange a vigil where at least two people, armed with digital recording equipment, sit at the haunted site and quite literally wait for something to happen. The vigil might take the form of a small séance where you as the ghost-hunter invite spirits to make contact. Although you as the leader of this particular investigation will be fully aware of the folklore surrounding the site in question, it's probably a good idea that others in the vigil party know as little as possible and go into the experiment with few pre-conceptions.

Ensure too that **evidence** collected during the vigil is not contaminated by over-elaboration. If, for example, a member of the party sees the apparition of an old soldier walking through a wall, he should not turn to a colleague and ask: 'Did you see the old soldier walk through the wall?' The best response would be simply to ask: 'Did you see that?' The colleague then replies with a simple 'yes' or 'no', again guarding against over-elaboration that might later be construed as auto-suggestion. Importantly though, both members of the vigil should make a note of the time of the conversation and record exactly what they did or didn't see.

If you see a ghost-hunter seemingly poking himself in the eye in a moment of high excitement during a vigil, don't be alarmed! An interesting theory supported by some in this business is that a ghostly apparition is genuine if, when you press very gently on one eyeball, you see a double image for a split second. If what you are seeing is a hallucination – a product of the mind – apparently you will only see a single image.

If you have a **medium** in your party it is fascinating to record his or her verdict on contacts made during the séance. Afterwards you can check the medium's connections and findings against established historical fact.

My view is that you cannot get closer to history than actually seeing a ghost. Parapsychologists take a different angle. They prefer in the first instance to talk to people who claim to have witnessed paranormal activity rather than attempting to experience the phenomenon themselves.

Whichever approach you choose to take, be as methodical and unemotional as possible. Your body needs to listen and work in a new way, so try to rest as much as possible in the hours before the investigation takes place. You will probably be up all night, so you will need all the energy and awareness you can muster. Don't confuse your body either by treating it to large doses of alcohol or a large spicy dinner before a vigil; eat sensibly and take along snacks that will give a kick to your blood-sugar levels during the night. Remember at around three o'clock in the morning the body goes into a different mode. This is the time when most people die and most people are born, and it is also the stage during all-night vigils that you need to give your body some fuel. Be as healthy as possible in body and spirit and be aware that even something as simple as a common cold can potentially confuse an investigation. Was that the ghostly tolling of a distant bell you just heard, or a buzz in your ears brought about because you blew your nose?

Many people like to take a **psychic** or medium on a ghost hunt. Do *not* tell them where you are going. Drive them to the location yourself, giving nothing away. You then need to measure exactly how accurate the psychic is. This can be done by creating a map of the location and recording the findings of more than one psychic at each point on the map. Alternatively draw up a list of emotive words, such as 'Happy', 'Angry', 'Murder', 'Child', 'Mediaeval' and so on… and ask each psychic to ring the words they feel most appropriate to particular areas of the location. If you discover that more than one psychic logs the same emotions in the same areas, then you are accumulating useful evidence of a haunting.

I believe the vast majority of psychics have an innate ability to see something the rest of us can't detect. It's a gift in the same way as someone who has the God-given talent to play a piano without music. I also know there are some complete charlatans practising as psychics, but I believe in ghosts and I believe in the supernatural, so I have to believe in mediums.

I have a party-piece when visiting, in particular, ancient sites such as castles, which demonstrates powerfully to me the energy that emanates from stone. I have a crystal on a string that I carry around with me and I have shown tens of thousands of people on my ghost walks how an ancient stone's energy can make the crystal swing on the string of its own accord. All I do is hold the piece of string with the crystal attached in one hand, and place the palm of my other hand on the stone. Within seconds the crystal will start to move – without any assistance from me – and I can only explain this as the energy transferring itself through my body, using the power of the mind. The moment I lift my hand from the stone, the crystal's gyrating action slows down and eventually stops. I don't cheat; I don't have to, and I defy anybody to come up with an explanation for this feat that doesn't have a supernatural foundation.

Before you read on, remember that most people who see ghosts aren't frightened when they see them, because the ghosts usually look like real people. The other important thing to remember is that eight out of 10 ghost stories can be accounted for; it's the other two you need to worry about!

So sleep well, and don't have nightmares.

GLOSSARY OF GHOSTLY TERMINOLOGY

Amulet is an item that has the power to stave off ghosts and evil spirits.

Angel is something often mistaken for a ghost, but in fact is a holy and protective messenger shielding us from harm.

Animal ghosts are believed to be the spirits of animals who survive the death process. Many experts in the paranormal acknowledge the existence of animal ghosts and some investigators even believe animals have what is known as a 'collective soul'. This theory supposes that as many as half a dozen animals at one time may share just one soul.

Apparitions are recorded in the earliest pages of history. This mysterious image of a disembodied spirit can be recognised as a human or animal. They are the most rare type of ghost to capture on film. Ghostly human forms are the easiest to fake, especially with the advanced technology of computers. This makes our job even more difficult, as it is almost impossible to prove the existence of apparitions when using photographs. Ghostly apparitions of ships, trains, cars and other inanimate objects have been seen. Some are said to appear to warn of a disaster that is about to happen, while others are thought to guard sacred places. Some apparitions are not seen, they are heard, or felt.

Apport happens when a solid object appears from nowhere, with the assistance of the spirit in the company of a medium.

Astral body is the energy that separates itself from the human form but still maintains the personality and feelings of the individual. Sometimes others will see them during an out-of-body experience (OBE) or a near-death experience (NDE).

Astral plane can be described as a level of awareness in the celestial world with its own standards and occupants.

Atmospheric apparition is a visual imprint of a person that has died left to be replayed on the atmosphere.

Aura is an energy field that surrounds all living things.

Automatic writing occurs when a ghost or spirit takes control of the writer's hand and pens a message.

Banshee is a spirit that appears before a person's death to howl a mourning song and to welcome them into the afterlife. It is also Ireland's most famous ghost. The correct pronunciation of this female spirit's name is 'bean si' and she is said to associate herself with Irish families – particularly if their surname starts with the letter 'O' – and she is more likely to be seen by a third daughter. Her appearance is said to be the portent of death for a family member, announced by crying and wailing during the hours of darkness. The sound is said to be like that of two cats fighting, only much worse. The tragic relative might be thousands of miles away in another country, and the wailing can apparently be heard for several nights in succession until the actual death occurs. The woman herself appears in contrasting ways. Sometimes she is described as a strange-smelling small, ugly hag dressed in rags. At other times she appears as a young and beautiful woman in a green dress, her eyes red and swollen from constant crying. A third type of banshee has also been reported, but it is not clear whether she is young or old, as she has no clear features, with holes where her eyes should be. The common factor linking all three types is very long hair that streams out in the wind. Folklore dictates that when a banshee is disturbed by a mortal person she will not appear again while that generation lives, but will return to haunt future generations.

Bi-location describes the phenomenon where someone can be in two places at the same time.

Birds were at one time believed to be messengers of the dead – when one tapped on a window, it was said to signify that a ghost was looking for another spirit to join it. Certain birds, such as sparrows, larks and storks, were said to transport to earth the souls of people from the Guff, or 'Hall of Souls', in heaven. Other birds, especially crows, were believed to carry the spirits of humans onto the next plane of existence.

Boggart is a word used chiefly in the north of England to describe a particularly nasty type of ghost. Boggarts are said to enjoy crawling into victims' bedrooms at night and pulling the bedclothes off, slapping, pinching and biting people, especially on the feet. In appearance they are said to be truly frightening, with sharp, long and yellowing teeth.

Bogies, like the Irish banshee, are said to make a wailing noise. An unpleasant spirit with a preference for haunting children, the bogie, according to British folklore, is foul-smelling, black, short and hairy with an ugly, grinning face. Perhaps it belongs more to the language of parents, hence the warning: 'Don't be naughty, or the bogie man will get you!' Bogies were once thought to be the most powerful of ghosts, having apparently once served the Devil by doing evil deeds against mankind.

Cats, next to dogs, are the most common form of animal spirits. The ghost cat is believed to have its spooky origin in ancient Egypt where cats were often worshipped, especially at Bubastis, where many thousands of mummified cats have been excavated. Historically the Devil was believed to be able to take the form of a cat, and cats were often thought to be witches' familiars.

Cemetery lights hover over graves after dark as bluish balls of light.

Channelling is a form of spirit possession that occurs with a medium who is communicating with an unseen entity to gain wisdom or gain knowledge of future events.

Clairaudience, a skill claimed by many mediums, is when someone has the ability to hear the voices of ghosts and other sounds that are inaudible to the human ear. These disembodied voices of the dead, or other entities, normally tell of events yet to happen. Many mediums say that they can hear dead relatives passing on information from a place they call 'the Spirit World'.

Clairvoyance is being capable of seeing events in the future or past through the mind's eye. In its simplest form, clairvoyance is to 'see with sight beyond the normal human range of sight'. A clairvoyant can see visions of events that have already happened, are actually happening or are yet to happen.

Clairsentience is, some believe, a basic human instinct finely attuned and polished. If you are clairsentient, you have the ability to feel and know things that have been, are, and are yet to be.

Cold reading is done when a psychic has no prior knowledge of the sitter.

Cold spot is an area in a haunted place where the temperature drops by several degrees. Temperature can also rise in heat by several degrees, indicating the presence of a fire in the past.

Collective apparition occurs when more than one living person sees a ghost or spirit simultaneously.

Collective unconscious is a term to describe a form of analytical psychology developed by Carl Jung. It represents the collective memory of all humanity's past and is held somewhere inside the unconscious mind.

Conjure is an act to summon a spirit to manifest itself for a desired task or to answer questions.

Corpse candle is a term referring to balls of firelight that can be seen to dance above the ground.

Crisis apparition is the vision of someone that will appear during waking hours or in a dream at the moment of a crisis.

Crossroad ghosts have been reported for centuries, and no-one knows quite why. Some researchers maintain that crossroads are more likely to be haunted because of the number of suicide victims buried there. The superstition behind interring the dead at such places lies in the Christian belief that the cross is a form of protection from demons, vampires and other supernatural night creatures. This theory, however, is thrown into doubt when it is considered that excavated human remains pre-dating Christianity have been unearthed near crossroads all over the world.

Deathwatch is a strange turn of phrase connected with a species of beetle known as the deathwatch beetle, which taps on wood. Many believe the beetle can sense the approach of death and taps in acknowledgement of spirits arriving to take the soul to its next destination.

Dogs have been reported in ghost form all over the British Isles. These spectral dogs are said to vary in size and some have been described as small but with extremely large eyes. They can also be white, black, vicious or gentle. The

Lancastrians have a ghost dog known as a Striker; in Wales there is the Gwyllgi, while Derbyshire boasts Rach Hounds and Gabriel's Ghost Hounds.

Doppelganger is a German word to describe a ghost that is the double of a living person. Those who experience seeing their double are said to be heading towards misfortune in the near future. Confusingly, other investigators are adamant that the doppelganger is also an indication of good fortune, though recorded incidences of them being a good omen are rare. People associated with the haunted individual are also reported as having seen the doppelganger at a place where the living counterpart was nowhere near.

Dowsing is the skill of seeking answers and interpreting them through the use of rods or a pendulum. Dowsing is widely used as a simple but effective way of searching for such things as lost coins, water and ghosts. It is also used to conduct geophysical surveys.

Drudes are mature witches or wizards, and reports of this nightmare ghost date from ancient England. The drude is said to be well versed in the art of magic and able to cause a ghost to appear in the dreams and nightmares of their chosen victims.

Duppy is the name given to a well-known West Indian ghost said to be able to walk the earth only between the hours of dusk and cock-crow. The duppy can be summoned from its grave by an act of ceremonial magic to do the bidding of a witch. The ceremony involves mixing blood and rum together with other substances. This concoction is then thrown on the grave of one known to have been an evil person when alive, as the duppy is widely believed to be the personification of evil in a human.

Earthlights are balls of lights or variable patches of lights appearing randomly and with no explanation as to what causes them.

Ectoplasm is a strange substance said to extrude from the sweat glands, mouth, nostrils and genitals of some mediums while in a trance-like state. A solid or vaporous substance, it is produced by a medium during a trance to reach a dead person. Ectoplasm, or teleplasm, is derived from the Greek words *ektos* and *plasma*, meaning exteriorised substance. There are researchers who claim that the substance is similar to pale white tissue paper, cheesecloth, or fine silk strands that all gather together to make a human shape. Others say the substance is like human and animal tissue. Most reports of ectoplasm have been revealed to be hoaxes. Some mediums have gone to the lengths of taking cheesecloth and rigging it to drop from a part of the body (the nose, mouth or ears). Some mediums even swallowed the cheesecloth and then regurgitated it later during the séance.

Ectoplasmic mist will usually show up in a photo as a misty white cloud to indicate the presence of a spirit. The mist is not seen when the picture is taken. These mists can vary in colour from grey and black to red and even green.

Elemental spirit is a rather curious type of ghost said to be a spirit that has never existed in human form. For this reason, occultists insist they are ancient spirits representing Earth, Air, Fire and Water that predate man. Elemental spirits are often associated with haunted stretches of woodland and rivers, mountains and valleys.

Elves are spirits of nature. Spiteful creatures, they are suffering as lost souls trapped between two worlds; not evil enough to go to hell; not quite good enough to be accepted into heaven.

EMF (Electro-Magnetic Field) meter is a device that can pick up electronic and magnetic fields. It can also detect any distortions in the normal electro-magnetic field.

Entity is a term that refers to an intelligent being who is no longer inside their physical body. They have the power to provide information to all individuals who are sensitive to their vibrations.

ESP (Extra Sensory Perception) represents an ability to gather information beyond the five human senses.

EVP (Electrical Voice Phenomenon or Electrical Visual Phenomenon) is a method by which a spirit's voice is detected by means of a recording device. It is also possible to pick up visual images of a known dead person on computer and TV screens, even when they are not switched on.

Exorcism is a religious ceremony where an attempt is made to expel a spirit that may have taken up residence inside a house or a human being. The ceremony usually involves a clergyman such as a priest, often specially trained, who will say prayers and repeat loud exhortations, often burning candles and sprinkling holy water while incense is burned. Exorcism is actually a modern version of the old Christian practice of excommunication – the rite of 'Bell, Book and Candle' – where sinners were eliminated from further entering the faith by a priest who would ring a small bell and slam the Holy Bible shut, often after reading the Malediction. The priest would then extinguish the burning candles. Modern mediums claim to be able to conduct exorcisms without the usual religious trappings by psychically contacting the spirit causing the problems and convincing it to move on to the next spiritual plane of existence. In some cases it is believed that ghosts in need of an exorcism are spirits that have not come to terms with their passing, especially where their demise has been untimely or tragic.

Exorcist is an individual – usually a religious holy man – who is skilled in removing demons from within people or locations.

Extras is a word used to describe faces or whole images of people that mysteriously appear on photographs. There are many reported instances of pictures revealing the image of a long-dead relative, or even someone still alive but living thousands of miles away, when they are developed. In the early days of photography, many of these wispy images were faked, but there are a small number of examples that defy explanation even today.

Fairies are tiny, invisible mythical beings. The pranks they play are sometimes mistaken for the activities of ghosts or poltergeists. Many types of fairies are believed to exist with each one being connected to an element, as in earth (Gnomes), fire (Salamanders), air (Sylphs), and water (Undines), and the colour green is apparently sacred to them. They are said to live in hills, valleys, among the trees and also where there are ancient burial mounds and ancient stone circles.

Family apparition is a ghost that haunts one particular family. When the ghost appears it is an omen that someone in the family is going to die.

Fireball is a Scottish phenomenon. Described as a medium to large sphere, it moves in a smooth and often slow way, most often over stretches of water. Fireballs are thought to be the souls of the departed returning to earth to guide the souls of people who have recently died to the next world.

Galley beggar is an old English ghost referred to as early as 1584 in Reginald Scot's work, *The Discovery of Witchcraft*. This ghost has the appearance of a skeleton and its name is derived from the word 'galley', meaning to frighten or terrify. The classic image is that of a screaming skeleton – head tucked under one arm – encountered on a country road.

Ghosts are different forms of apparitions of deceased human spirits that can appear to any of our five senses. They can be seen as a shadowy human or animal form. They can be heard and may even emit a familiar or offensive odour. They are trapped between worlds.

Ghost buster is a specialist in clearing an area of ghosts, poltergeists, spirits or other haunted activity.

Ghost catcher is a type of wind chime that will clink together as a ghost wisps by.

Ghost hunt describes a conscious effort to search out a known ghost or to visit other places suspected to be haunted.

Ghost-hunter is a person who seeks to find ghosts or haunted places and tries to determine what type of spirit activity is taking place, and why.

49

Ghost investigation involves going into an area looking for ghosts or hauntings under controlled conditions. Reports are made to document the events. Listing all the reading of the equipment along with time, weather, and temperature as the project unfolds becomes valuable information for the research.

Ghoul is a grotesque, evil spirit with a terrifying face that gains its sustenance by robbing a grave to eat the flesh of the recently deceased. The ghoul was at one time the common word for a ghost in Arabia.

Graveyard ghost is a ghost believed to have special abilities. According to folklore, the first person to be buried in a churchyard was believed to return to guard the site against the Devil. Because this task was so great, a cat or dog was often buried before any human, so it would become the guardian of the dead and remain so until the Crack of Doom.

Gremlins are a recent phenomenon, originating from World War Two in 1939–45 when pilots flying dangerous missions reported seeing strange goblin-like creatures in the aircraft with them. A 'gremlin in the works' is common parlance now for when machinery grinds to a halt.

Grey lady is said to originate from Tudor times. Some say it refers to the ghost of a woman who has been murdered by her lover or one who waits for the return of a loved one. There's another theory that these ghosts represent the Dissolution of the Monasteries, which resulted in the death of many monks and nuns, who would have been dressed in grey habits.

Hallowe'en can be traced back long before the advent of Christianity. Our ancient pagan ancestors celebrated the 'Feast of the Dead' by lighting great bonfires across the country to summon the dead and placate them by offering burnt sacrifices. The Christian Church is thought to have moved the bonfire tradition to 5 November, marking Guy Fawkes's fate, in an attempt to dilute the true meaning of the night. Modern witches still celebrate the night of 31 October by holding feasts and performing magic rituals. According to legend, Satan opens the gates of hell at the stroke of midnight and all spirits of evil are set free to wreak havoc on earth. By cock-crow these spirits must return to hell, where the gates are slammed shut at the first sight of dawn. Any spirit left outside would disintegrate forever.

Haunted chair is an essentially English phenomenon referring to people who have a fondness for a particular armchair coming back as a ghost and being seen in the same chair.

Haunt is the place where the ghost or spirit continues to return. Ghosts usually haunt places and not people.

Haunting is used to describe the repeated display of paranormal activity in a particular area. Some hauntings are thought to be poltergeist energy from a disembodied entity trapped in a certain location or by the energy left behind from a very strong tragic event or accident. Occasionally, hauntings appear to be an intelligent ghost trying to make a connection with someone on the earthly plane to give a message. People can also be haunted, as can any item that may have belonged to someone deceased.

Headless ghosts are the spirits of people whose death occurred because they were beheaded. There is also evidence to suggest that these types of apparitions may be connected to the ancient practice of beheading the corpses of people suspected of being connected in life with witchcraft and sorcery.

Headless horsemen in ghost tradition are believed to be the results of riders who may have been ambushed and decapitated while riding at speed through wooded glades. Another theory is that headless riders are ancient chieftains who lost their heads in battle and still wander the earth in search of their dismembered heads.

Iron is believed to be a sure antidote against all kinds of bad magic and evil spirits.

Lemures is the Roman word given to evil ghosts who return to haunt relatives and friends. Ceremonies to placate these spirits were often held in ancient Rome.

Ley lines are the invisible lines that run between sacred objects or locations.

Luminous body is the faint glow in a dead body to signify a soul's impending departure.

Malevolent entities are angry spirits, often seeking revenge. They sometimes attach themselves to a living being, causing them discomfort and distress. They tend to impose their anger or depressed personality on the human being they possess.

Materialisation is the ability claimed by some mediums to bring into vision a spirit or ghost. One of the first recorded incidents occurred in America in 1860 and was performed by the Fox sisters, founders of modern day spiritualism.

Medium is someone who can communicate with the dead. During a trance state the medium allows the spirit to take over their body so they can deliver a message to the living. The medium does not remember any of this once they come out of the trance. Today the new mediums refer to this as channelling. The big difference is that nowadays the medium remains completely conscious of what he/she says and experiences through the spirit.

NDE (near-death experience) is when a person dies and is revived after a short period of time. The person remembers their death experience and can recall visions of the afterlife, which include ghosts and other paranormal events. Survivors of this experience say it changes their whole outlook on death and they feel as if they can live better lives after this realisation.

Necromancer is a person considered to be a sorcerer or wizard, who has the power to raise the dead and force the spirits to obtain information about the future.

Orbs are globe-shaped lights of energy caught on film, usually during a haunting or other paranormal experience. Orbs are believed to represent the spirit of an individual that has died. They are made up of the energy force that powered their body in life. They may vary in size, colour and density.

Omen is a prediction of a future event.

Oracle is a prophet that can communicate with spirits, ghosts and gods to obtain information.

Ouija Board is a board with cards of numbers – zero to nine – the letters of the alphabet, and the words 'yes', 'no' and 'goodbye' printed on the surface. A glass beaker or wine glass is placed on the table and the consultation can then begin. The board comes with a planchette (a pointer) and once you lightly place your hand on it the pointer will spell out the answers to the questions asked by the players. This 'game' can be dangerous if participants are not fully aware of what they are doing and are not educated in psychic science.

Paranormal is any experience that happens beyond the range of scientific explanation or normal human capabilities, including hauntings, telekinesis, telepathy, clairvoyance, or any other rarity that cannot be justified by the five senses.

Perfumed ghosts manifest themselves in the form of a scent. Many people have experienced smelling the favourite scent of a deceased relative, such as an aunt or grandmother.

Phantom coaches are also known as 'death's messenger', and are apparently seen in silent progress before a death in the family. The horses are always said to be headless and the coaches are described as black and sometimes have the appearance of a hearse. The skeleton-like driver is usually viewed as horrendously ugly, with a fixed grin.

Planchette is a pointer used with an ouija board to communicate with spirits, ghosts, or entities of a higher plane.

Poltergeist is a noisy and sometimes violent spirit. While ghosts haunt and like solitude, poltergeists infest locations and prefer company. The name 'poltergeist' means 'noisy ghost'. Known traits of the poltergeist are banging, thumping, moving objects, levitating, and causing fires. These same results can also be attributed to an unconscious outburst of psychokinesis. More researchers of today feel that much reported poltergeist activity is related to psycho-kinesis rather than a ghost.

Possession is when an evil entity takes over a human body and forces the soul out. This allows the spirit to use the host by exerting its own will. This may totally adjust the host's current personality. Women aged under 20 are most commonly attacked in this way and show clear signs of emotional distress. The discarnate spirit seeks out humans to display emotions of anger, revenge and resentment.

Precognition is the foreknowledge of future events.

Psychic is a person who tunes into phenomena beyond their five senses and has the ability to see or sense the future, present and past. The talents of a psychic include but are not limited to hearing voices, seeing spirits and knowing what might be happening in the future. Unfortunately these gifts have been misinterpreted as mental illness for some. Psychics have also been referred to as seers or sensitives.

Psychokinesis is the ability to move objects using only the power of the mind.

Psychomancy is the ancient art of reading future events through the appearance of ghosts, interpreting what their manifestations to the living might mean.

Purgatory is the place where the souls of the dead must go to be cleansed of all their sins before being allowed into heaven, according to Catholicism.

Reciprocal apparition is an experience where the individual and ghost see and react to one another.

Reincarnation is the belief that once a person dies their soul returns to a new body where it will continue to learn lessons about life and how to reach enlightenment. Many reincarnations may be necessary for the soul to learn and become closer to the goal of perfection.

Retrocognition is the foreknowledge of past events.

Salt, according to ancient customs, is an antidote to all manner of witchcraft and evil spirits. It is said anyone carrying salt in his or her pocket is protected, even against the Devil himself. Placing salt in every corner of rooms in a haunted building is also said to subdue wicked spirits.

Scrying is a form of divination in which an individual stares deeply into an object such as a crystal ball, mirror or flame, in order to see an image that might appear. Such images – usually generated by a spirit – can be symbolic and give answers to a question.

Séance consists of a group of people sitting in a circle holding hands in the hope of contacting the dead. The procedure is conducted by a medium that goes into a trance, as a vehicle for the deceased spirit to take over and communicate with loved ones, sometimes through a spirit guide. Knocking or rapping sounds can also be heard during a séance. The word is of French origin, meaning 'a sitting', and there's no limit to the number of participants, though even numbers apparently get better results.

Sensitive refers to a person who can detect paranormal events beyond the range of their five senses.

Shaman is a medicine man or witch doctor who can communicate with the spirits during a trance and who also possesses the power of healing.

Sixth sense is to have the power of perception in addition to the five senses. It is also a popular term for ESP.

Smudging is a form of cleansing or clearing a spirit from an area by using incense to purify the area.

Spectre is most commonly used now to describe a ghost that is faked or the result of natural factors.

Spirit guide is a heavenly spirit or guardian angel that is present and offers help to the individual to which it is attached. This help may be a simple feeling that comes over the person when they need guidance for a problem or situation. Some people claim they can communicate with their guides at all times.

Spirit photography is usually a photo that contains a face or form believed to be that of a deceased person.

Spiritualism is a belief structure that assumes that spirits and ghosts can communicate with the living.

Supernatural is when an unexplained occurrence take place out of the realm of the known forces of nature. The experience usually involves spirits.

Table-tipping (typology) is a type of communication with the spirit world by using a table. Participants start out with any size table and surround it with a number of people. Everyone places all five fingers lightly on the table. All together the group chants, 'Table up, Table up'. Usually the table will start to quiver or lift to one side. If someone in the group has strong energy the table might rock back and forth or lift off the floor. At this point a question may be asked with a response from the table tapping, once for 'yes' and two for 'no'. If there is a non-believer present the table will probably not move. This type of entertainment can be dangerous and is not recommended to those not skilled in psychic science.

Talisman is a protective charm or amulet said to have the ability to ward off evil.

Telekinesis is where a person can move an object through the power of thought without physical means to move the object.

Telepathy is a method of communication from mind to mind, sometimes across great distances.

Teleportation happens when an object is transported from one location to another by disappearing and then reappearing in a different place.

Time slips occur when the past and present collide at a location.

Trance, a state between being asleep and awake, is where a medium uses his or her body as a channel for waiting spirits to pass messages through to living relatives and friends.

Transmigration is the belief that a soul can move from body to body through the process of reincarnation.

Vassage is a spirit that inhabits a scrying crystal. During a scrying session, the spirit communicates by forming literal or symbolic images.

Vengeful spirits return from the dead to avenge terrible wrongs that have been done to them.

Vortex is a small tornado-shaped image that shows up on pictures when there is a spirit present. Orbs can apparently be seen rotating inside the shaft. Sometimes the vortex is so dense it will cast a shadow. It is believed that the vortex is a means of travel for spirits in the orb form.

Wakes are a noisy ancient custom of watching over the dead while vast amounts of alcohol are consumed. This tradition, especially popular in Ireland, is based on the theory that drinking – as alcohol is a cleanser – helps the spirit of the deceased on its journey to the next world. Music, singing and laughter are encouraged, as it is believed loud noises keep evil spirits at bay.

Warlock is often used to describe a male witch, but this is insulting to many so-called warlocks, as the word has been used in the past to describe a traitor.

White ladies have been seen all over the British Isles, traditionally haunting castles, mansions, halls and even bridges and stretches of water. In ancient times, pagans, to give them a safe passage, apparently sacrificed young women to river gods.

Will-o'-the-Wisp – also known as jack-o-lantern, ignis fatuus, corpse candle and foolish fire – is a ball of flame that floats in mid-air. Such phenomena have also been observed bobbing or dancing just above the ground in yellow and blue flames. These wondrous episodes have been recorded since Roman times. The Native Americans believe them to be a fire spirit warning everyone of danger. The Germans thought the balls of flame were lost or trapped souls that couldn't move on. In Africa some believed that the Will-o'-the-Wisps were witches trying to scare sinners into behaving properly. In Russia, these lights represent the souls of stillborn infants. Throughout Europe when these lights appeared it was thought to be evil spirits that couldn't enter heaven but were not evil enough to be condemned to hell. It would be foolish to follow these strange dancing lights.

Witch is a person – particularly a woman – who practises witchcraft. Most worship nature, but there are different types. Most modern witches would not use their powers for evil, preferring to help human, animal and spiritual awareness. An unwritten law is that witches cannot reveal to anyone what they are or how they practise their art in the belief that silence is power, and power brings knowledge.

Wizard is someone with remarkable abilities and usually proficient in the art of magic. Most male witches prefer this title.

Wraiths are claimed to be the ghost of a person on the edge of death whose appearance should be seen as a warning to the witness that their days are numbered.

PART TWO

THE GHOST
TOUR OF
GREAT BRITAIN

DERBYSHIRE

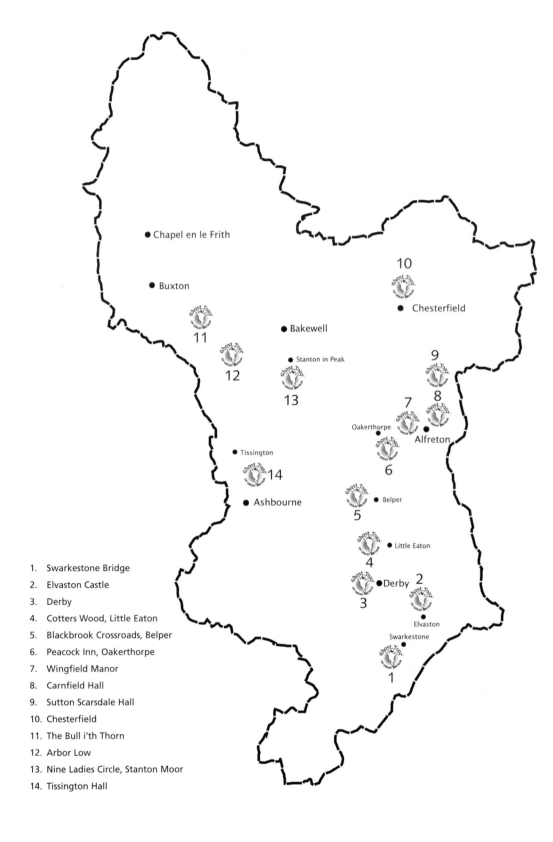

- Chapel en le Frith
- Buxton
- Bakewell
- Stanton in Peak
- Chesterfield
- Oakerthorpe
- Alfreton
- Tissington
- Ashbourne
- Belper
- Little Eaton
- Derby
- Elvaston
- Swarkestone

10
11
12
13
7
9
8
6
14
5
4
2
3
1

1. Swarkestone Bridge
2. Elvaston Castle
3. Derby
4. Cotters Wood, Little Eaton
5. Blackbrook Crossroads, Belper
6. Peacock Inn, Oakerthorpe
7. Wingfield Manor
8. Carnfield Hall
9. Sutton Scarsdale Hall
10. Chesterfield
11. The Bull i'th Thorn
12. Arbor Low
13. Nine Ladies Circle, Stanton Moor
14. Tissington Hall

INTRODUCTION

Blessed with stunning vistas, Derbyshire in the full pomp and
splendour of a clear day can be breathtakingly majestic.
However, this East Midlands county can also be an
inhospitable place, certainly during the winter months, and
its bleakness has contributed to Derbyshire's many myths
and legends. In bygone days, farmers and villagers in the
high-ground settlements in the northern reaches of the
county tended to be holed up and saw only near neighbours
and their own families for weeks, sometimes months, on end.
It was only with the first signs of spring, when the snow, rain
and winds had finally faded away, that these hardy people
emerged into the market towns with their tales of terrible
hardship borne through the dark days of winter. Mixed into
these colourful stories were strange happenings, the telling
of which has been handed down the generations as folklore.
So we have the country folk of Derbyshire to thank for many
of its eerie legends.

Derbyshire is a ghost-hunter's paradise, a place ripe with
legends of goblins, witches and boggarts. Its ancient standing
stones emit an inexplicable energy that still captivates people
today, while prehistoric trackways and leylines leading
through the county are the perfect backdrop for mythology to
thrive. Make no mistake: Derbyshire is a very haunted place.
So settle back and let me take you on a tour of one of this
country's most haunted counties.

Bordered in the north-west by Cheshire, in the north by
Yorkshire, in the east by Nottinghamshire, in the south by

Leicestershire and in the west by Staffordshire, my home county measures 52 miles from north to south, and for most of that length it is only about 20 miles from east to west.

Although the city of Derby is by far the largest settlement in the county, other towns of importance include Alfreton, Ashbourne, Bakewell, Belper, Buxton (England's highest town), Chesterfield, Glossop, Heanor, Ilkeston, Long Eaton and Matlock. From the hedgerows and arable fields of the south of the county to the dark peaks of the north with its seemingly endless miles of dry stone walls and rocky pastures, Derbyshire boasts a rich variety of customs from the earliest times, together with stunning panoramas set against a breathtaking milieu of hills, dales, rivers and magnificent country houses such as Chatsworth, Kedleston Hall and Haddon Hall.

Its reputation as a most haunted county is accentuated by the isolation of some of the towns and villages, many of which were constructed centuries ago from the plentiful native stone. Add to this a proliferation of remnants from the ancient past, including burial mounds or 'lows', which crown so many hills in Derbyshire, and the scene is set for an area of central England loaded with paranormal activity. Among the county's mysterious prehistoric monuments are the Arbor Low stone circle and henge near Hartington and the atmospheric Nine Ladies stone circle on Stanton Moor, north of Matlock. Both are featured in this book.

Britain's first National Park – the Peak District – is situated in Derbyshire and is the very stuff of legend. It was designated in 1951 to celebrate spectacular, unspoilt, often stark scenery. The Peak Park covers 555 square miles of the north of the county, taking in the limestone plateau and dales of the White Peak and the brooding gritstone moors and edges of the Dark Peak. It speaks volumes for the haunting beauty of the Peak Park – and the description is deliberate – that today it is the second most-visited National Park in the world.

Away from the remoteness of the north, Derbyshire's central and southern regions are steeped in history, not least because of the role they played in the shaping of Britain's Industrial Revolution. The importance of the Derwent Valley mills is recognised worldwide through its status as a World Heritage Site. Snaking down the Derwent Valley from Matlock Bath to Derby and taking in Sir Richard Arkwright's groundbreaking Cromford mills, this area of Derbyshire was at the heart of the development of the factory system, helping to shape modern society as we know it. The site includes a series of mill complexes, river weirs, mill settlements and an historic transport network.

I have personally visited every haunted place described in this book of Derbyshire ghosts and the accounts are made entirely from my own observations and those of the *Ghost Tour of Great Britain* team, from conversations with trustworthy individuals who have the mixed blessing, through a trick of ownership or stewardship, of living with the dead and the weight of history.

I

SWARKESTONE BRIDGE

Situated in south Derbyshire, Swarkestone Bridge is a very famous historic site. I had a cairn erected here in 1995 to commemorate the farthest point south reached by the Jacobean Army of Charles Edward Stuart, known of course as Bonnie Prince Charlie. Aiming to reclaim the throne of England from King George II for his father, the prince carried the hopes and aspirations of the Stuart family. In 1745 the bridge at Swarkestone was the only crossing point of the River Trent between Burton and Nottingham. Crucially for the prince's army it was also the only way to London and possible victory. But it was at this bridge on 6 December 1745 that word of a retreat was relayed to the 70-strong advance cavalry. The long trek back from Derby to Scotland began, ending in bloody defeat for the Highland Army at Culloden on 16 April the following year.

Swarkestone Bridge is also special because it is the longest stone bridge in England – almost a mile long – and it continues almost as far as Stanton by Bridge. It was built in the 13th century and there's a special myth associated with its construction. Two beautiful sisters – the Bellamont girls – were betrothed to marry two local knights. One stormy evening these men were called to a meeting with barons on the other side of the River Trent. This meeting coincided with a very special party organised by the Bellamont girls to celebrate their forthcoming weddings. Determined to attend the party when their meeting ended, the two knights made it

THIS CAIRN MARKS THE
FARTHEST POINT SOUTH REACHED
BY THE JACOBITE ARMY OF
PRINCE CHARLES EDWARD STUART
ON 4TH DECEMBER 1745

Erected by the
Charles Edward Stuart Society
& Marstons Brewery
on the 250th anniversary

Photo: D. Redfern.

back as far as the banks of the Trent, which, after incessant rain, was in flood. Foolishly they led their horses into the fast-flowing torrent and although their steeds tried valiantly to get across to the other side, they were swept away and the knights drowned.

Heartbroken, the Bellamont sisters devoted the rest of their lives to raising money to build a causeway over the river, so no other soul would have to face the devastation of losing a loved one to the unpredictable Trent. They gave so much of their money to this end that they died in penury and the Bellamont sisters were buried in the same grave at Prestwold Church in Leicestershire. On wild nights, when the Trent is swollen, it is said that the sisters' ghosts can be seen looking

in vain for their lost loves who were so tragically drowned in the river's gloomy waters.

So undoubtedly, Swarkestone Bridge is a place of death, tragedy and of battle.

A gentleman walking his dog across the bridge reported that he heard the clatter of hooves and the jingling of cavalry accoutrements, but he could see nothing. What he thinks he sensed was the cavalry of Bonnie Prince Charlie's Highland Army. In fact it is equally possible that these were soldiers from earlier times. This same site was the scene of the 1643 Battle of Swarkestone Bridge during the Civil War, when a skirmish took place between the troops of Oliver Cromwell and King Charles I. Bloody fighting took place, with soldiers being thrown off the bridge to certain death in the fast-flowing waters of the Trent.

The nearby Crewe and Harpur pub has been the site of an inn for the past 800 years and people sitting in the picturesque beer garden on a summer's evening have heard the clamour and clatter of battle at the nearby Swarkestone Bridge. But I know of no one who has ever actually *seen* anything strange on the bridge. So what have people heard? This is a substantial stone bridge and the sounds that people have picked up fit perfectly with the stone tape theory, which dictates that traumatic death can be recorded in stonework. I certainly believe that at this ancient bridge and causeway we are hearing the clamour of earlier times, of tragic and traumatic death, being played over and over again at certain times on the anniversary of a major event, or when the climate allows.

2
ELVASTON CASTLE

Five miles south-east of Derby is the imposing Elvaston Castle. One of the many stately homes still preserved in Derbyshire, Elvaston was designed by James Wyatt and built around 1817 for the 3rd Earl of Harrington. The estate belonged to the Stanhope family until the mid-20th century when the then Earl of Harrington sold the estate to the local authorities. However, the site actually goes back to the time of the Vikings when it was known as Elvostune. Elvo the Viking lived here many years ago, so the 1817 castle is built on top of much earlier foundations.

In fact, if you take a closer look at Elvaston you will find it still contains a wing that dates back to the16th century. The

Photo: D. Redfern.

difference in the brickwork is evident and I challenge anyone stepping into the Elizabethan wing not to sense the dramatic change in atmosphere. It is here, in this 500-year-old section of Elvaston Castle, that the ghost of a lady, wearing white, has been seen through a particular window. Witnesses have glanced up at this window and seen the shadowy figure of a white lady moving slowly backwards and forwards as if she is sitting in a rocking chair. Others have seen a misty apparition making its way along the pathway that leads from the castle to the church and the churchyard. For this reason, no one is quite sure if the white lady is a castle ghost or churchyard ghost, because she has been seen in both locations and also passing between them.

Though the building itself is splendidly imposing, the grounds are the greater glory of Elvaston. The beautiful 200-

acre park was landscaped in the 19th century. Neglected for many years, it was rescued in the late 20th century by Derbyshire County Council and it is rightly famed for its long avenues, serpentine lake, a Moorish temple and the large and unexpected example of rocaille. The gardens also boast golden gates from a French royal palace. Originally there were 11 miles of evergreen hedges, an Alhambra garden, a French garden and others. Botanical expert J.C. Loudon, in 1839, noted, 'The solemn gloom cast over part of the grounds by these yew trees produces an effect never to be forgotten, which harmonises with the fine old ivy-covered church adjoining the castle.'

Photo: D. Redfern.

77

In broad daylight the churchyard at Elvaston Castle can be a peaceful haven, a retreat from the hurly-burly of 21st-century life. The splendid tombs of the Harrington family can be found here, in the shadow of the castle, including Canova's beautiful monument to the 3rd Earl, who died in 1829. At dusk, however, the ambience of this final resting place of the great, the good and the not so good, changes.

The churchyard, the burial place of the Earls of Harrington, is set within the grounds and the first thing that greets the visitor is a rather sinister gravestone that reminds us of our frail mortality. In memory of Stephen Allcock, who departed this life on 18 September 1842, it features a chilling inscription that reads: 'I once did stand as thou dost stand now and viewed the dead as thou dost me. Ere long thou would lie as low as I and others stand to look on thee. So bring thought.'

Mausoleums can be both fascinating and daunting. Stone coffins and their grisly contents, displayed in full view, somehow bring the harsh reality of death into sharp focus. In the churchyard at Elvaston there is a family crypt where all the Earls and Duchesses of Harrington are buried. All, that is, except for one. On the other side of the graveyard, not even within the shadow of the mausoleum, is an interesting grave. This final resting place is beyond the boundary even of the graveyard, which is fringed by a yew hedge. Accessed through a gap in the hedge and overgrown with weeds and nettles, it is the grave of a Harrington not afforded the reverence of being allowed to rest in peace in the family crypt. This is the grave of Kathleen Emily, widow of Dudley Henry Eden, the 9th Earl of Harrington. She was born on 4 November 1862 and died at the grand old age of 86 on 6 August 1949. Kathleen Emily was the wife of the Earl of

Harrington, but why is she buried outside the graveyard? Was there a family rift? Was she estranged from her husband? More to the point, why was she buried the wrong way round? The traditional Christian method of positioning a coffin or shroud-covered body in a grave was to have the body with the head to the west, feet to the east. The body was placed face up. When it was not practical to use the west-east position for a grave, a north-south position was the next best option and, if this were the case, the body would then be laid on its side, head to the north and facing east. Not all burials followed the tradition, nor did all cemeteries, but it seems that Kathleen Emily's grave has been deliberately positioned differently to the other graves in the graveyard.

Normally the reason for misalignment was that the east was determined by the position of the sun on the eastern horizon at sunrise at the time of the establishment of the burial ground. It was the *perception* of east that set the direction, not the compass.

Photo: S. Lilley.

It is therefore not surprising that the ghost of a white lady – thought to be Kathleen Emily Harrington – is seen at the dead of night, wandering around the graveyard. She has been seen stopping and looking at different gravestones, shaking her head. Perhaps she is not resting because she is not in the graveyard near her husband or in the Harrington family crypt. Perhaps she is lamenting the fact that her remains have been deliberately misaligned. No one knows.

So while the lead-lined coffins of the Earls and Duchesses of Harrington are perched on shelves in full view through a window of the mausoleum, Kathleen Emily rests uneasily, it seems, in her lonely grave nearby.

The Happy Huntsman's Tree

Next to the grave of Kathleen Emily at Elvaston is the Happy Huntsman's Tree. One Earl of Harrington was a famous foxhunter killed in a hunting accident in February 1917. His hounds weren't brought out again for ages, but in his Will he

Photo D. Redfern.

Photo: D. Redfern.

left a statement that his hounds should at least be let out to hunt on Boxing Day every year. When Christmas came, these instructions were carried out and the hounds were let out of the stables at Elvaston, but the dogs simply ran round and round the Happy Huntsman's Tree and wouldn't move. There was nothing, apparently, that the huntsmen could do to get the hounds to come away from the tree. It is said therefore that the ghost of the Earl of Harrington haunts the tree.

3

DERBY

Derby is the country's most haunted city, and I have written extensively over the years about the ghosts to be found here. For the purposes of this book, which covers the whole county, I have chosen just a few examples – there are many more to discover if this whets your appetite!

Scream, Friargate

While on my tour of the city of Derby, I visited Friargate, and found myself at the aptly named Scream, a student club. This was originally, in 1230, a Dominican Friary, hence the name Friargate for the road, but when the monasteries were

Photo: S. Lilley.

dissolved in the 1530s it became redundant and was eventually knocked down and replaced with a huge 48-bedroom Georgian mansion, built here in 1725.

The building has rather small cellars for a place this size, and there is a very good reason for that. When builders were digging the foundations they started unearthing all manner of human remains including bones and skulls, as well as lumps of wood from coffins. They stopped work and, consulting old plans, found they were digging in an area marked *Ye Friars' Graveyard*. Consequently the place was sealed off and never excavated any further.

Perhaps this disturbance of human remains is why Scream and Friargate in general are so haunted. The cellar at the Scream is a place packed with paranormal activity. Some of the rooms are haunted too, while spectres of friars have been seen in the bar area. Apparently they return to see what has happened to their beloved friary.

I have visited this particular place, formerly known as the Friary Hotel, many times and in my opinion it is one of the best-preserved Georgian buildings in the centre of Derby, complete with its beautiful 18th-century panelling. Unfortunately the bar has changed quite a lot, but it was here one Friday night many years ago in the 1950s that a gentleman called David, who was the under-manager at the hotel, was sitting with five other men. All were perched on bar stools when all of a sudden the temperature dropped and each man was pushed over like a row of dominoes, one on to the other, beer flying everywhere. The unfortunate last man actually fell off his stool because there was nobody for him to fall on to, and he broke his elbow! The drinkers then noticed that moving away from them was what looked like a monk, wearing a black hood and a black cloak. To their collective

amazement, it disappeared through the oak panelling at the end of the room. What David thinks he saw was probably not a monk, but a friar. Dominican friars wore black and were known as Black Friars.

But if the bar has its own stories to tell, it's downstairs in the cellars under the old Friary that evil seems to lurk. The things that go on in there you wouldn't believe! The cellar corridor is actually part of the original friary going back to 1230. The walls are original and visitors can see one of the original mullioned windows of the old friary with the centre-piece and the old original bars intact. Continuing down, the cellar gets very low. Thankfully there are lights, but in the dark this place would feel extremely unwelcoming. I walked to the very end, as far as the cellars go, and I reached the point where we know bodies are buried. I was down among the dead men, in the part they were digging out in 1725 when human remains and bits of coffin started falling out.

For obvious reasons, this cellar is one of the spookiest places on my Derby ghost tour, and the number of incidents that still happen to unwary visitors down here is truly alarming. On one of my tours two ladies were pushed over in one of the cellar rooms and lights, mostly green and similar to will-o'-the-wisps, have appeared when the lights were switched off. Although I believe that generally speaking ghosts prefer not to appear when there is an audience, down in the old friary cellars it seems to be a different story.

Not long ago, an electrician, working alone with his torch in the property in an unlit room next to the old friary cellars, had a frightening experience. He was feeding wires through from one side of the building to the other through holes in the wall and sensed there was something in there with him. He carried on working, but the unnerving feeling that he wasn't alone prevailed, and eventually he turned around and, to his horror, saw a friar wearing a black hood standing in the corner of the room. This spectre had no face and the electrician immediately dropped his tools and ran, not daring to return. He was so shaken by his experience that his company had to transfer him to another job in Nottingham!

Although the cellars of the old friary must be the scariest part of the property, there's also a haunted bedroom – the infamous Room 106. It was in this bedroom in 1850 that the son of a mayor of Derby shot himself and his ghost is said to haunt the room to this day. There's a marvellous story from several years ago connected with a wardrobe in this bedroom when it was a hotel. A businessman staying here walked into the room at about three o'clock in the afternoon to freshen up during a busy day. He was amazed to find all of his clothes had been taken out of the wardrobe and were lying on his bed. He didn't think anything spooky was going on and instead went downstairs to reception to complain. Staff asked him which room he was in and when he replied 'Room 106', they said, 'Oh yes, perhaps we could move you to another room, perhaps an upgrade.' He said he didn't want to move, he simply wanted an assurance that no one would come into his room and disturb his clothes. That night, he was woken from a deep sleep at half past three in the morning to find both water taps running at full blast in his wash basin and, the next moment, both wardrobe doors flew open and his clothes came out on to the bed. Within minutes he was downstairs in reception, empty suitcase in one hand, his clothes in the other, on his way out!

I also caught up with two employees at Scream, Sarah and Adie, who told me a story about one of the girls there who trained members of staff all over the country. During a three-day training course in Derby she needed somewhere to stay and opted for the old Friary Hotel. She too was awoken in the middle of the night and saw, hanging with chains from a roof beam, a half torso. She still works with staff at Scream from time to time but refuses point blank to sleep in the building, preferring to check in somewhere else.

The door in Room 106 is also said to always open by itself. Staff check it every day and although it is on a proper latch it always seems to be open by at least a couple of inches. The taps in the bathroom still come on by themselves, and this phenomenon actually happened when *Most Haunted* filmed here. The room was checked before filming began: lights in the room were turned on and the door was locked. However, when a member of staff returned to check all was well, it was absolutely boiling in the bathroom and full of steam. The hot tap was all the way on, and it had to be twisted a couple of times to turn it off. Someone had turned it on and the only person who could have been in the bedroom was one of the old spirits who live at the old friary. Sarah also told me how half a dozen staff members staged a séance in Room 106 one night. All stood around a table and one person asked if there was anybody there. The sign the party asked for was for the table to move if the answer was affirmative and indeed the table started to move across the carpet. Sarah, who was taking part, suspected at first that someone around the table was responsible for moving it, but, as the table started to move around at will, she became convinced that a supernatural power was in the room. A couple of weeks later we tried to film the room using a night vision camera. We had 90 minutes of battery life on the camera when we first went into the room, but three minutes of power disappeared instantly. During filming, I asked questions of the spirits in the room and, playing back the tape, we saw lots of orbs, as many 30 or 40, moving around the table.

The resident DJ at Scream stays in a room a couple of doors up from the haunted Room 106. While in bed he has heard footsteps outside in the corridor at dead of night. When a camera was placed in the hallway one night, it captured a multitude of orbs and the sound of a bang was heard, and people walking.

The beauty of the old friary is that it is active, and inexplicable things are happening every day and this makes it a very special place. It's a haunted property that doesn't rely simply on old stories. The great thing is that because it is open to the public as a student club and restaurant, people can go in, day and night, and enjoy the spirits behind the bar!

Vernon Gate

Vernon Gate at one time boasted the third county gaol, which was built at Derby in 1828. It was in its day the most modern prison in England. Executions took place here from 1833, either from the top of the Gate House or in front of a window where a gallows was set up with a trapdoor that opened to a drop of 17 feet above the streets.

All condemned prisoners had to step out on to this gallows and, in 1862, Dick Thorley, who had cut his girlfriend's throat in Agard Street, stepped out to be hanged by William Calcraft. This supreme executioner, with 45 years of service, was the longest serving hangman in British history. Thorley became a victim of Calcraft after murdering his girlfriend in a frenzied attack. He had heard she was two-timing him and in April of 1862 Thorley went to visit her and, when she started taunting him, he grabbed a cut-throat razor from his pocket and slashed her across the neck. As she collapsed to the

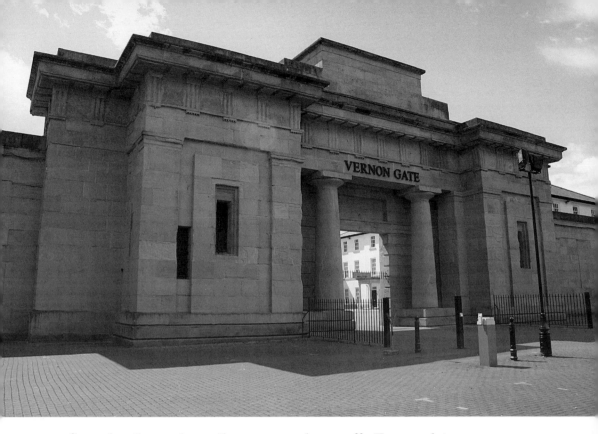

Photo: S. Lilley.

floor, he threw down the razor and ran off. He was later arrested and sentenced to death. So Thorley stood on the trap

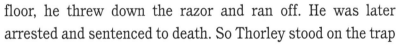

Photo: S. Lilley.

door, a white cap pulled over his face and the noose adjusted around his neck. Calcraft then pulled the lever and launched him into eternity. After hanging above the street for the customary hour, Thorley's limp body was taken down and a plaster cast – a death mask – was made of his face. He was buried in a lime

pit in a local graveyard, which his ghost is said still to haunt to this day. I went to see where this graveyard once was and it was easy to imagine all the executed men and women in makeshift coffins lined up against a wall, where they were buried at right angles.

Thorley, along with many other people, all condemned to death and hanged at Vernon Gate, was buried under where my feet were. I know that Thorley's ghost is often seen wandering along a little passage that I later walked down, close to where the County Gaol had been, wearing a white cap over his face with a rope around his neck. How people know it to be Thorley I don't know because the ghost's face is covered by a mask, but I presume it is due to the fact that Thorley is the most infamous person to be buried here. Why? It is because here in 1862, a remarkable 20,000 people turned out to watch Thorley as the star of the show in Derbyshire's last public execution. Thorley's girlfriend, Eliza Morrow, is also said to haunt the area. I have spoken to no fewer than 20 women, all of whom claim to have seen Morrow's ghost wandering around Longden's Mill, where her house used to be.

Hive Recording Studio

This is an extremely interesting story. Next door to Derby Gaol is a building now known as the Hive Recording Studio. A few years ago a lady rang me to say that her son had seen a ghost here at the Hive Studio. It was about 10:10pm on a Sunday night and he was working there as a member of a pop group called the Bee Keepers. As the keeper of the keys, he was the last one out that night and, while locking up, he heard a loud jangling of keys, so loud that it shocked him and hurt his ears. Thinking no more of it, he put his keys in his pocket and started to walk down the alleyway next to the studio. Coming towards him was a big man wearing a long trench coat tied with a belt. Our man became alarmed because it became clear that this figure seemed set to attack him. The figure continued to advance, staring into our man's face. Trying to defuse the situation, the Hive key-keeper asked the figure if he was alright, but received no reply, only a hard stare as it continued to advance. He expected to get thumped, but the figure went straight through his right shoulder without him feeling anything and continued up the alleyway. At this point there was a loud clang, as if a metal door had closed, and the figure vanished. Our man, exhausted by this terrifying experience, slumped down, shaking, in a heap by the wall and was found here by an elderly lady. She said she had seen the man attack him and asked if he was all right. He explained that the spectre in the trench coat had actually walked straight through him before vanishing halfway down the alleyway. Needless to say, he returned home and poured himself a stiff whisky.

No one else has reported seeing a ghost in this area since. Perhaps the properties backing onto this alleyway were once cottages belonging to the gaol and that is the

Photo: S. Lilley.

significance of the keys and the slamming of a metal door, I don't know.

What I can't do is prove these ghost stories. All I can do is relate to you the stories that I have been told; the rest is up to you. However, I know full well after years of talking to and interviewing people that people have been scared by what they think they have seen. Some perhaps have vivid imaginations and others may have had too much to drink. But the one undeniable fact is that people *do* see ghosts.

The Blue Lady of St Werburgh's Church

When Miss Jenny Nichols received her set of colour prints from a photographic studio she was shocked to see a blue shadowy figure in the foreground of a picture she had taken inside the 14th-century St Werburgh's Church, Derby, in

1976. She was shocked because she could categorically state that when she took the photograph there was absolutely nothing in her viewfinder but the church's interior. In my opinion this is one of the few photographs of this type that appears to be absolutely genuine. I have seen many examples of ghostly images that I reckon have probably been tampered with,

Photo: D. Redfern.

93

but the Blue Lady at St Werburgh's seems to be the real thing. It is reputed to be the ghost of Elizabeth Gilbert, wife of Henry Gilbert, the Squire of Locko Park. Her stepmother was Shakespeare's granddaughter.

When I first started to research the Blue Lady of St Werburgh's all I held as evidence was a faded newspaper clipping from the *Derby Evening Telegraph*. However, I have now seen the original 1976 photograph and I am 100 percent confident it is the genuine article. My colleague Steve Lilley has a lot of experience in the manipulation of photographs through his work as a professional cameraman. He took the original piece of celluloid film from 1976 and scanned this into a computer. Using magnification, immediately we could see an arm, a dress and a head. Tweaking the saturation up also enabled us to see that the apparition is transparent with a hazy blue glow around her. Back in 1976 the technology to fake photographs simply didn't exist. All the pixels are the same shape and the same size and Steve is convinced it is not a fake. Because we have seen it on film we have the evidence that it hasn't been manipulated using a scalpel or by overlaying one picture on top of another.

Such were Elizabeth Gilbert's achievements in life that a monument to this great lady can be found in St Werburgh's Church – and those who look hard enough might also catch a glimpse of her ghost.

Farm cottage poltergeist

There's a wonderful farm cottage on the outskirts of Derby that dates back to the 1680s. Apart from its age, it has nothing to recommend it in terms of known connections with historic events or any major disturbance. However, this Derbyshire cottage is a perfect example of how a seemingly ordinary private house can in fact be out of the ordinary because of the inexplicable things that happen there. Filming part two of my *Derbyshire Ghosts* DVD I visited this house, where the occupants, Clive and Kelly, had reported poltergeist activity. They had no axe to grind with anyone and were certainly not publicity seekers, but strange happenings in their home had made them so desperate they had asked three priests to come out to do an exorcism.

Steve the cameraman and I arrived ahead of the clergy to be told by the couple that a local priest had already told them that an earth-bound spirit was haunting their home. This priest had blessed the house, but had warned this would either give the spirit a way out, or irritate it. Unfortunately, in this case, the poltergeist became very irritated indeed. It reached the stage where, when objects inexplicably started to move around in the cottage, Clive only felt safe in the house when he had his dog at his side – until the dog itself started to act very strangely too!

The poltergeist activity became so serious that Clive and Kelly moved out for a while before taking the bold step of moving back to their cottage in the hope that the poltergeist might have moved on. Their hopes proved ill founded, however, and one morning, soon after their return, Clive descended the staircase from his bedroom and walked into the kitchen to find the entire contents of a fruit bowl had been deposited near the dog's bowl. Bizarrely, five oranges and a bunch of six bananas had been lifted out of the fruit bowl. Could the dog have done it? Clive says not, as the dog never climbed on furniture. To have managed to dislodge the items of fruit without disturbing anything else on the table would have made this a very dainty dog indeed, especially as a bunch of six bananas would be a heavy load for an animal to carry in its mouth. To add to the mystery, there were no bite marks on the fruit.

In fact the dog, which slept in the kitchen, was an early clue to the haunting. Animals are usually more sensitive to ghosts than human beings and, thinking back, Clive recalls that his dog had showed signs of being petrified by something a long time before he and Kelly started to take note of the strange goings-on. Night after night it scratched and tried to get out of the kitchen and Clive couldn't understand why. Later he felt bad about his lack of sympathy for the poor animal and recalls that his response to its frantic scratching in the middle of the night had been to lock the dog in the kitchen. The dog's behaviour became even more peculiar. Of an evening it would settle down next to the log burner in the cottage and then suddenly, for no apparent reason, fly out of its basket and jump onto Clive's knee, or simply bolt out of the room.

If the dog was demonstrating its superior sensitivity to supernatural happenings, Clive and Kelly didn't have to wait long before the poltergeist made its presence only too plain. Above the mantelpiece the couple had a fine picture but one evening at about 9pm, when Clive was standing at the kitchen table, he heard a strange noise. Hearing it too, the dog suddenly scampered away and Clive was frozen to the spot in panic, as he saw the picture start to sway from side to side before suddenly slamming down to the floor. He recalls now that the dramatic effect was akin to someone throwing a brick through a window and the picture hit the floor with such force that glass splinters from its frame flew into the next room. Close scrutiny afterwards revealed the string hadn't broken on the back of the frame.

This description is typical of poltergeist activity. While

Steve and I were chatting with Clive and Kelly, we had to stop filming abruptly because the three clergymen arrived to carry out their exorcism. They told the owners of their own past experiences, perhaps in an attempt to put the couple's minds at rest, but Clive admitted later that he found their accounts quite disturbing. The clergy had brought along holy water from the font of their church and they sprinkled this throughout the house and blessed the occupants. They then offered the spirit guidance by advising it to 'go to the light'. However, they couldn't guarantee to Clive and Kelly that their intervention would work for the better. They told the couple that the spirit might now rest and follow the light, but it was just as likely if they were dealing with an earth-bound spirit with unfinished business that it would probably stay. If this was the case, the clergymen said they would have to return to force out this mischievous and frightening Derbyshire cottage poltergeist.

4

COTTERS WOOD, LITTLE EATON

Only two miles from the centre of Derby is the haunted Cotters Wood at Little Eaton. It sits high above the village, overlooking the primary school. Here in a hollow in the 1800s lived a farm labourer and his wife and the remains of their cottage can still be seen on the fringes of the wood. One morning the labourer left for work as usual, leaving his wife making cakes in the cottage. It was the last time he would see his beloved wife alive, for during the morning robbers attacked the cottage, killed the woman and stole what they could of value before making off. The labourer returned home that evening to see the door of his home wide open and blood still trickling down the doorstep. Stepping inside, he found his wife had been battered to death. The shock was too much for him and he ran away from the horrific scene and climbed the nearest high tree – an old oak that still overlooks the village to this day. Tying a rope to the boughs at the top of the tree, he threw himself off a high branch and hanged himself. It is said it took him more than 20 minutes to die from slow strangulation and, unsurprisingly, his ghost still wanders Cotters Wood. It is said that soon after his suicide the leaves at the top of the oak tree turned black and formed the shape of a hand pointing towards the cottage where his wife had been so cruelly murdered. The boughs at the top of the tree also apparently withered and died. I have to say that due to

Photo: S. Lilley.

the density of Cotters Wood it is not a pleasant place to be, even in daylight. Courting couples and people walking their dogs on moonlit nights have reported hearing the spine-chilling sound of a rope creaking backwards and forwards on a bough at the top of this ancient oak tree at Little Eaton.

5

BLACKBROOK CROSSROADS

This is a true story recounted to me by a gentleman called Mike Woodhouse, a well-known fruiterer who had a business in the centre of Derby and lived at Blackbrook, near Belper. One summer morning in August 1992, Mike was driving home on a road close to his house. It was broad daylight, about 11.30am. Approaching a bend in the road he saw a lorry coming the other way and also noticed a horse with a rider on it, dressed in black, in front of him. The rider was wearing a tricorn hat and had a long cloak draped around his shoulders. This was a big clue, but maybe Mike simply assumed the rider was an actor taking part in a film shoot. Anyway, he didn't question what he was seeing and pulled into the side to let the lorry pass by on the other side of the road. Mike noticed by this time that the horse and rider were also now on the other side of the road, lurking by a large tree. More concerned about the lorry, he then glanced away, but when he looked again for the horse and rider, they had disappeared. When he reached the junction of the main Ashbourne to Belper coach road – known as Blackbrook Crossroads – Mike looked again for the horse but couldn't see it anywhere. The highwayman and his steed had simply vanished. He thought no more of it and pulled across the road, continuing up Dally Lane to his house. He mentioned in passing to his wife that he had seen a horse and rider in old-fashioned clothes, but thought no more about his experience.

However, driving from his home at 5.30 one morning three weeks later on his way to the wholesale market in Derby, Mike reached the crossroads and, to his shock, directly across the road where there is a huge stable block, he saw the black-clad figure of a man sitting on a black horse. The spectre was wearing a tricorn hat and, once again, had a long black cloak slung over his shoulders. Mike stared in disbelief at the apparition and, on closer scrutiny, realised to his horror that the highwayman had no face. It was a truly frightening experience, especially as the last thing on his mind at that time in the morning was paranormal activity on a road near his own home. Confused, Mike drove on to Derby and tried to put what he had seen to the back of his mind. However, the following week on a Wednesday morning at 5.30 the highwayman again appeared at the crossroads. On this occasion, as he drove up to the crossroads, Mike sensed something was about to happen. He was so concerned on seeing the ghost that he immediately locked the doors of his Range Rover. Peering out through his windscreen he studied the highwayman in minute detail and satisfied himself that

Photo: S. Lilley.

what he had witnessed on the previous occasion was true: this shadowy figure had no face. Just as quickly as it had appeared, the highwayman disappeared.

Mike Woodhouse is a very down-to-earth bloke and not the sort of person who would readily attribute strange happenings to the presence of a ghost. He would certainly not fabricate a story such as this. In fact Mike declined to be interviewed on film for my *Derbyshire Ghosts* DVD series because he didn't want the publicity.

Crucially, Mike is not the only person to have seen a highwayman here. Could this be the spectre of Dick Turpin, who has also been seen on his horse Black Bess near the Peacock Inn at Oakerthorpe and on the Chevin? The Black-brook Crossroads is a dangerous road, and there have been a series of unexplained accidents here. One motorist skidded and drove into a wall of an old coaching inn near the cross-roads early one morning and he was killed. The police can't explain why he lost control of his car and we will never know what he did or didn't see that might have caused him to crash.

Steve Lilley, producer of my *Derbyshire Ghosts* DVD series, once lived near Blackbrook Crossroads in one of a row of old cottages. Returning home late one night after a night out on the town, he waved off the taxi that had brought him home, only to be confronted by a man who seemed to be wearing an 18th-century costume. The figure demanded to know where he had been that night, but Steve shrugged him off, assuming he must be a re-enactor taking part in a Murder Mystery event. However, making enquiries the following day, Steve discovered there was no such event in any of the neighbouring cottages. To this day Steve cannot explain the identity of the spectre that confronted him that night near Blackbrook Crossroads.

6
THE PEACOCK INN, OAKERTHORPE

The community of Oakerthorpe, a mile north of Alfreton, is situated on one of the oldest Roman roads in England and dates back to the 14th century. The settlement was known at one time as Ulgurthorpe and, unusually for its size, this relatively small mid-Derbyshire village can today boast three fine inns. For its most haunted reputation, it is the Peacock Inn that stands out. Dating back to perhaps the 11th century, this watering hole is referred to in the Domesday Book as Ufton Barns. Before it was a coaching inn, the Peacock was a monastery. Reputedly Derbyshire's oldest inn, it was rebuilt in 1613, became a popular changing post for carriages and has a strong connection with Dick Turpin and his legendary mare Black Bess. Cock-fighting would in bygone days have

been a popular sport inside the inn, but the Peacock also at one time harboured a dark secret – an underground stable near a blacksmith's at the rear of the premises, now filled in. It is known that local horse thieves hid horses temporarily in the secret subterranean stable. Legend has it as well that the ultimate highwayman, Dick Turpin, used the stable to hide his precious mare Black Bess. Locals say they have seen the ghost of Turpin in the bowels of the Peacock.

Although this underground stable has been filled in, other tunnels still lurk beneath the Peacock, and this is the haunted part of the building. White monks administered Ufton Barns, not far from Wingfield Manor, and one of the tunnels underneath the Peacock apparently leads all the way to the manor where Mary Queen of Scots was held captive in the 16th century. If this was built as an escape tunnel for the tragic Mary Stuart, then it didn't work.

I get very nervous of enclosed spaces, particularly haunted ones, and it was with some trepidation that I descended the stairs into the cellars of the Peacock Inn with my cameraman Steve. To start with, it just looks like any other cellar, nothing to get excited about at all, with nicely whitewashed walls. Nothing to worry about that is until you turn a corner and see the barrel-vaulted section, from where you have to feel your way through a small gap that takes you straight down into the inky blackness of the tunnel that leads to Wingfield Manor. It's wet, smelly and downright unpleasant down there and this is the place where the ghost of a white monk has been seen. So this expedition is not for the faint hearted, because you never know who – or what – you might meet coming the other way. Prepare to get very damp too, because this cut-away to Wingfield Manor floods on a regular basis. White monks dug out the tunnel originally in the 1400s, probably as a coalmine, and many are known to have died in rock falls as they carried out their backbreaking task. Some were left to rot where they were crushed and several people have reported seeing a monk with no face hovering above the ground. It's no surprise then that there are very few members of staff who will go down into the manor tunnel alone. Glasses have been known to fragment for no reason in the inn itself and on my first trip underneath the Peacock my candle flickered and went out inexplicably. There was no draught of any kind and when the flame died I didn't like it at all. I re-lit the wick, but almost immediately the candle went out again and I have to admit I couldn't muster the enthusiasm to go any deeper into the tunnels. In fact I will go so far as to say that my jaunt underneath the Peacock Inn has to rate as one of the most frightening since I started hunting ghosts.

For this reason, with great reluctance, I decided to return to the Peacock for the second DVD in the *Haunted Derbyshire* series. On this occasion I was better prepared with a pair of

Photo: D. Redfern.

wellies and a bigger candle. The fact that something uncomfortable happened to me in the Wingfield Manor tunnel on my previous visit made it very difficult for me to go back, because, as I have said before, I am genuinely afraid of ghosts. The landlord of the Peacock furnished me with a bit of Dutch courage in the form of a stiff brandy before I once again tackled the cellar steps. I really was extremely apprehensive about returning to the tunnel.

I knew that the rock I was tentatively touching as I made my way down again into the tunnels would have been hewn by the 14th-century Oakerthorpe monks with cleavers, axes and chisels and as I got deeper in I really began to feel incredibly scared. The previous time I was there my candle twice went out but this time my heavy-duty candle stayed alight – for a while. The further down I went, the damper and muddier it became until eventually I reached a parting of the ways where the way ahead seemed to be blocked. One route was completely silted up, while the other had been hit by a rock fall. It was while I contemplated what to do next that my candle suddenly went out. There was no discernible draught whatsoever and as I reached for my backup torch I have to admit that my heart was beating very fast indeed. Determined to plough on along the tunnels where ghostly figures of monks have been seen, I was stopped in my tracks as my candle again expired. Feeling ever more nervous, I found new tunnel entrances until I could get no further because of the mud. By then, I really had had enough. I didn't see any white monks in this ancient tunnel, but my candle went out twice, just as before, and it was time for a sharp exit. At the top of the tunnel I was brave enough to switch off my torch to see what this subterranean lair looked like in total blackness. It was only at this point that I noticed that the EMF meter I was carrying in my inside pocket had disappeared. It is a very deep pocket and I really can't understand how it could have dropped out – but somehow it had. Strange things had previously happened with this particular meter. A couple of days before I had placed it on a table in a haunted cottage and, with no one near it, the meter went off on its own. Now it had slipped out of a very deep pocket.

Years ago, while launching a *Ghost Tour of Great Britain* DVD at the Peacock Inn, I had another spooky experience here. A photographer from the *Derby Evening Telegraph* turned up for this PR exercise and couldn't understand why his camera kept running low on battery power. In total he used eight batteries during the photo-shoot and he told me this sort of thing had never happened to him before. I believe spirits – which need energy – were responsible for draining his batteries.

Under glass on the floor of one of the pub's lounges punters can view an illuminated section of the Peacock's secret tunnels and there's a skeleton in full view. Although this particular skeleton is plastic (I think!), delve a little deeper and I have no doubt genuine human bones still lie, as they have done for many centuries, below rock-falls and tons of silt beneath the Peacock Inn.

7

WINGFIELD MANOR

Near the Peacock Inn and situated only a few miles east of the very centre of Derbyshire, Wingfield Manor is a huge, ruined country mansion built in 1440 by Ralph, Lord Cromwell, Treasurer of England. Mary Queen of Scots was imprisoned here in 1569, 1584 and 1585 and although it has been unoccupied since the 1770s, the manor's late-Gothic Great Hall and High Tower remain. There are few finer specimens of the highly ornamented embattled mansions of the time of Henry VII and Henry VIII, a halcyon era of English architecture marked by a transition in style from castle to palace. I can think of no other place in the whole of Derbyshire whose weathered walls have so many wonderful tales to tell.

Though privately owned, English Heritage administers the manor house and, charmingly, it features a working farm within its grounds. Originally it consisted of two square courts and a noble hall, which was lighted by a beautiful

Photo: D. Redfern.

octagonal window and a range of Gothic windows. A rich Gothic window lights part of the chapel remains and the great State apartment.

Wingfield Manor's association with Mary Queen of Scots is still very much a talking point among locals today. Yet it was well over 400 years ago, in the 33rd year of the reign of Henry VIII – he of the many wives – that Wingfield Manor was in the possession of the Earl of Shrewsbury. In the time of Henry's daughter Queen Elizabeth I, Shrewsbury held in his custody at Wingfield the unfortunate Mary Stuart.

Born at Linlithgow Palace on 8 December 1542, Mary became Queen of Scotland only six days later. News of his daughter's birth came while her father, James V of Scotland, lay dying in Falkland after his defeat at Solway Moss. He never saw his daughter but uttered the famous prophetic words: 'It cam wi a lass and it'll gang wi a lass.'

By this James V meant that the crown of Scotland had come through a woman, Marjorie Bruce, and would be lost through a woman. At the age of six her French mother, Mary of Guise, sent Mary to France and in April of the year 1558, still only 15 years old, she married the Dauphin Francis, secretly bequeathing Scotland to France. In July of the following year Francis became King of France and, although she was still Queen of Scotland, Mary also took the title of Queen of France. However, it seems her thirst for queenly titles knew no bounds and soon she wanted to take over England. Her claim to the English title was based on her relationship as granddaughter of Margaret Tudor, sister of Henry VIII. Although Mary had fierce competition in the shape of Elizabeth I, the Roman Catholics of the land backed her claim because they rejected the Virgin Queen's lineage in the belief that Henry VIII's marriage to Elizabeth's mother

Anne Boleyn was illegal. Mary returned to Scotland following the premature death in 1560 of her husband, Francis, after 17 months on the throne. In Scotland, she married her first cousin Henry Stewart, Lord Darnley, on 29 July 1565, but the union quickly soured and Mary turned to her Italian secretary, David Rizzio, for comfort and advice. On 9 March 1566, when Mary was six months pregnant, a group of Protestant lords, acting with the support of Darnley, murdered Rizzio in the Queen's presence at Holyrood Palace. She survived the horrible ordeal and in Edinburgh Castle on 19 June 1566, estranged from her husband and his allies, she gave birth to a son James (later James I of England).

By the end of that year, Mary had befriended James Hepburn, Earl of Bothwell, and on 10 February 1567 Darnley was murdered at Kirk o' Field. The circumstances of his death remain a mystery to this day. The chief suspect, Bothwell, was acquitted after a brief trial and on 15 May 1567 he and Mary were married according to the Protestant rite. This alienated some of Mary's closest supporters and the nobles of Scotland combined to face Mary and her new husband at Carberry. The Queen was forced to surrender, and Bothwell fled. Mary was imprisoned at Lochleven Castle and on 24 July 1567 she was compelled to abdicate in favour of her son, who became King James VI of Scotland. With the help of a few brave friends, Mary escaped from the castle and immediately rallied a

Photo: D. Redfern.

large force behind her. They engaged in battle at Langside on 13 May 1568. Easily beaten by the army led by the Protestant lords, Mary left Scotland and headed for England to beg support from her cousin Elizabeth.

But her flirtation with England – much of it centred on Derbyshire – was a sad story of incarceration and, eventually, execution. As Mary crossed the Solway into England she could not have suspected that she was offering herself up to nearly 19 years of captivity. She never returned to Scotland and, while incarcerated in England, she was the subject of numerous escape plots hatched by English Roman Catholics and foreign agents. The chief of these focussed on the Babington family of Dethick, a small community three miles from Wingfield Manor.

Mary's suite of apartments at Wingfield Manor was on the west side of the north court, perhaps the most beautiful part of the building. It communicated with the Great Tower, where, it is said, the captured Mary sometimes had the opportunity to see friends approach. Her incarceration at Wingfield started in 1569 and in that same year an attempt was made by Leonard Dacre to rescue her. After this, Elizabeth I became suspicious of the Earl of Shrewsbury and directed the Earl of Huntingdon to take care of the Queen of Scots in Shrewsbury's house. In consequence, her train was reduced to 30 people. Her captivity at Wingfield is stated to have extended to nine years, but it is known she also spent time in Buxton and at Chatsworth during this time.

Whenever she was at Wingfield, legend has it that Sir Anthony Babington, a young Catholic idealist who saw Mary as a martyr, would dress as a gypsy to gain access to the manor grounds, crushing walnuts and smearing the oil onto his face to create a weatherworn impression. He would

Photo: D. Redfern.

apparently climb the walls of Wingfield Manor to visit his
heroine. However, her 'keeper' by this time, Sir Francis
Walsingham, had access to Mary's 'secret' correspondence
with Babington and, unfortunately for both Mary and Sir
Anthony, one of Babington's letters mentioned the ambiguous
removal of Queen Elizabeth. Prompted by the bitter
disappointment of those long years of illegal imprisonment
and her son's betrayal, she replied, approving Babington's
plans. With relish, Walsingham drew the sign of the gallows
on this last letter and Babington was immediately arrested
and executed.

Although reluctant to execute her cousin, Elizabeth
eventually gave an order that was carried out in grisly
circumstances at Fotheringay Castle on 8 February 1587.

Mary was buried first at Peterborough, but in 1612, after he had ascended the English throne, her son James had her interred in Westminster Abbey.

Hers was a most horrendous execution, so is it any wonder that Mary Stuart is still said to wander the grounds of Wingfield Manor? She came down the main staircase of Fotheringay Castle dressed in black and removed her garb to reveal a crimson petticoat, the sign of a Catholic martyr. A handkerchief was tied around her eyes and she knelt with her head on the block. The executioner's first blow bit into the back of Mary Stuart's neck but did not kill her. She turned her head towards him and whispered, 'Sweet Jesus'. The executioner ordered her to put her head back on the block but still, even after the second blow from his axe, it was not properly severed. The executioner had to cut the last sinews of Mary's neck with his pocket knife before triumphantly holding the head aloft and declaring: 'So perish all enemies of Elizabeth!' But, shockingly, the royal head then dropped out of the red wig Mary was wearing and bounced across the scaffold floor. Her lips are said to have continued to quiver for a quarter of an hour after her execution. Illuminated by a candle, the head of the Queen of Scots was placed on a huge platter in one of the windows of Fotheringay Castle as final proof that Mary Stuart was dead.

The crypt at Wingfield is the most haunted part of the manor and the ghost of Mary Queen of Scots has been seen in this ancient undercroft, as has that of Anthony Babington. She died because of a man from Derbyshire called Anthony Babington and both their ghosts still linger at Wingfield Manor – united in death, as in life.

The ghosts of other worthies probably wander the ancient ruins at Wingfield. The mansion was ravaged during the Civil

War in the reign of Charles I after being possessed by Royalists. It was besieged and taken by Lord Grey of Groby and Sir John Gall of Hopton, brave officers in the service of Parliament who began their assault on the east side from Pentrich Common. Using cannon, they soon opened a considerable breach in the wall, captured the

Photo: video still.

place, and Colonel Dalby, who was the governor, was killed in the siege. Maybe Dalby's ghost rests uneasily at Wingfield, for, disguised in the dress of a common soldier, he was recognised by a deserter and shot in the face as he walked in one of the stables.

Sitting on top of a hill in Amber Valley, Wingfield Manor is one of the real gems in Derbyshire's crown. Haunted by plotters, monks and Royalists, it is a wonderful place to visit.

Photo: D. Redfern.

8

CARNFIELD HALL

For pure atmosphere, the 15th-century Carnfield Hall – situated on the B6019 road between Alfreton and South Normanton – takes some beating. Fine oak-panelled rooms create a perfect haunted house backdrop at Carnfield, which was extended during the 16th and 17th century and restored in the early 1990s. The fine interior, including a 16th-century Great Parlour, a Georgian dining room and two impressive Jacobean staircases, has a blend of styles from its Elizabethan origins to more recent times.

In the late 1950s Carnfield Hall was unoccupied and

Photo: S. Lilley.

derelict. Mining subsidence had caused severe cracking and the house was abandoned. Even in its dilapidated state, the Hall was a magnet for unexplained occurrences. On numerous occasions in the 1960s and 1970s, passers-by would report that the derelict property was on fire, only for police to arrive to find nothing more sinister than the aroma of candles. It is said too that an old gentleman of the road reported in those derelict years that he made a mark on the gate of Carnfield as a signal to other tramps that it was haunted and, however welcoming it might look from the road, it should definitely *not* be used as a night time resting place.

In 1987, under threat of demolition and after standing derelict for 30 years, Carnfield was bought by James Cartland and he spent a considerable amount of time and energy restoring it and researching its history and wider connections. The Cartland family were Birmingham industrialists in the 19th century and the house now features many family heirlooms.

It is known that a house stood on the Carnfield site from earliest times, but the current Hall, built as the Manor House

Photo: S. Lilley.

of South Normanton, was started in the 15th century. During the following century a local family – the Revels – took up residence and incredibly were associated with Carnfield until the early part of the 19th century. In their 300 years at Carnfield, the Revel family regularly changed and extended the property, building the great staircase in 1620 and a Georgian front in 1698. It was at this time that some of the old mullioned windows were replaced by the fashion of the time – timber-framed sash-weighted windows. However, some original mullion windows survive on the south face of the Hall. In addition to Cartland family heirlooms, Carnfield contains a fascinating collection of house documents dating back to the 16th century, antique furniture, porcelain, glass, family portraits, needlework and even old costumes and toys, including a lock of Edward IV's hair, Princess Charlotte's wedding stockings and Louis XIV's travelling trunk, together with collections of antique fans, silhouettes, snuffboxes and local archives.

From this description and its many centuries of occupation by high-powered families, it is easy to understand why, in my opinion, Carnfield is one of the most haunted places in Derbyshire. James Cartland has told me many stories of hauntings at the house. He admits most are unproven, but I believe where the same legend is handed down by different generations, there must be a grain of truth in the origin. There is rarely smoke without fire.

Inside this building, which has so many tales to tell, a shadowy figure has been seen at the bottom of the main staircase. James Cartland himself has heard strange noises at dead of night and numerous visitors have sensed something unnatural about the Hall. There are definitely cold spots and, alone in the house, James has heard footsteps on the staircase, which dates back to 1627. Consider all the Derbyshire people who have walked up and down these stairs across the centuries in their farthingales and tricorn hats. Maybe some of them are still doing it!

The Great Parlour would originally have featured a smoky fire at its centre and rooks would fly freely around the open space up to the roof. In Elizabethan and Jacobean times the fashion was to lower ceilings and it would have become a living area where ladies would embroider and great parties would be held. A few years ago a team of well-known ghost-hunters set up some machinery and recorded harpsichord music being played very faintly. This instrument was identified by an expert as a rare organ harpsichord – the Rolls-Royce of harpsichords. James Cartland later found an inventory from 1727 that included an organ harpsichord, an expensive wedding gift, dating back to 1666. It was given by Sir Nicholas Wilmot to his daughter, who married Sir Francis Revel. Maybe the reason it was heard so faintly on the recording was because the instrument would have been played in the dining room, a little distance from the Great Parlour where the recording was actually made.

Recently a TV crew, filming outside the Hall, directed their cameras into the Great Parlour through a window and when the film was looked at the editor discovered shadowy hands, raised in gaiety as though a dance was taking place there, on the recording. Legend has it that Carnfield is the scene every year of a Ghostly Ball that commemorates the greatest night in the Hall's history – a party to celebrate Robert Revel's appointment as High Sheriff of Derbyshire in 1700. On another section of the TV crew's film, taken through a different window, the shadow of a man's hand, with a great lace cuff, was found.

Robert Revel's portrait still hangs in the house and his name appears in an

Photo: video still.

old family tree dating from the early 1700s. This document states that his servants murdered him in his bed in June 1713 or 1714. All his papers have disappeared and it's a story no one knows anything about. At some stage during his tenure though, we know he decided to turn the House around, effectively declaring that rooms previously at the back of Carnfield were now at the *front* of the Hall. Perhaps this is the reason that when James Cartland first moved in he regularly heard the sound of furniture being hurled around in Robert Revel's bedroom above. Sometimes this happened twice in a month, and then there would be no activity for up to six months. However, so eerie and troubling was this that James had the bedroom blessed, and no unnatural noises have been heard since.

In recent years, a group of psychics who knew absolutely nothing about Carnfield as a house of murder visited and on inspecting Robert Revel's bedroom, all came out holding their chests, claiming someone had been suffocated in there. It makes sense that anyone committing a murder at dead of night would use suffocation as a neat form of doing away with the lord of the manor. It would have been a clean death, certainly less messy than a stabbing, and who knows, maybe the robbers finished off poor Robert Revel with a bed bolster.

Carnfield has existed for at least 500 years and although James Cartland will tell visitors that, to his knowledge, no strange happenings have been reported in the Great Hall, outside it is a different story. Several people have seen the ghost of a gamekeeper who walks in the park. Local families have either seen him or have been told of sightings by family members going back several generations. There's also a ghostly coach and six, typical of Jacobean times, which apparently still makes its stately way down the original old drive at Carnfield. Another popular sighting outside the Hall is that of three children playing on one of the lawns. Three separate people, all of whom had relations who were servants at Carnfield in the 19th century, have told James Cartland that the ghost children had been seen on occasions by grandparents and great-grandparents. Apparently the servants, many of them maids, would gather in the gardens at Carnfield on summer evenings at dusk. Here several witnessed the three ghost children playing bat and ball and all were consistent in their description of two little girls and a boy in a tricorn hat. The children appeared in misty fashion, played bat and ball, and then simply dissolved away. The boy, James Cartland believes, is Tristram Revel, and the girls are his two sisters. Colonel Tristram Revel, Adjutant of the Derbyshire regiment, was the last in the long line of Revels and when he died at Horsham, in Sussex, in 1797, he left no children and the estate was passed down to the son of his benefactor, Sir John Eardley Wilmot, the Lord Chief Justice. The Wilmots, however, never lived at Carnfield and a lawyer, William Wilson, managed the estate. When the Hall was eventually put up for auction, it was acquired by Joseph Wilson of Chesterfield. Arrested later on fraud charges, Wilson died in Derby Gaol, but Carnfield remained in the family, being passed to his daughter, Isobel, who married Thomas Radford of Smalley Hall in 1829. The estate was inherited by their son, Vaughan Hobbs Radford, who lived at Carnfield Hall until his death in 1912, when the house was in some need of renovation.

Bought the following year by a local estate agent, Mr Melville Watson, the Hall was treated to some necessary improvements, but this work came to a sudden halt when Watson was shot dead by one of his tenant farmers during an argument. The tragic Watson's widow carried on living at Carnfield until 1949 when it was sold to Mr Derbyshire, a local businessman, before falling into disrepair.

James Cartland is the 20th generation of families that have lived at Carnfield since 1475 and the days of Dame Alice Babington, the same Derbyshire family that was involved in the Babington Plot.

There's also a portrait in the house of Frances Revel, who was only 20 when she died in a smallpox epidemic in 1736. Although she died in Nottingham, Carnfield was her family home. She was recently married and at the Hall her love letters are on display, together with a pocketbook that lists all her expenses. We know she played the spinet, loved painting and drawing and she had a pony called Dimple. James even has the bills for its hay.

In the south-east bedroom there is said to be a white lady who walks through a blocked-up door. Women visitors continue to see the white lady to this day, and James's mother has witnessed it too. However, it is always women and never men who see her. The blocked up door would once have led to a dressing room and then into a maid's bedroom. Whether she is an old maid – an aged unmarried member of the family – or a servant maid, we don't know. But, unnervingly, guests have awoken in the middle of the night to find her standing by the side of their bed.

A great example of how a building can retain something from the past in an altogether natural way can be found on one of the ancient windowpanes in a bedchamber at Carnfield Hall. On it is scratched the words: 'Robert Revel of Carnfield'. This Robert, the uncle of the ghost children so often seeing playing bat and ball on the old House's lawns, died in 1729.

9

SUTTON SCARSDALE HALL

How many people have driven down the M1 and seen Bolsover Castle on one hill and opposite it the gaunt ruin of Sutton Scarsdale Hall? Built in 1724 by Smith of Warwick, this 18th-century remodelling of an earlier house is now in ruins, but visitors can see the fragments of its former rich plaster decoration. Once one of Derbyshire's finest houses, it was built for the first Lord Scarsdale, who is supposed to have been the model for the old peer in Hogarth's *The Rake's Progress*. A later owner was thought to have been the inspiration for the character Sir Clifford Chatterley in D.H. Lawrence's novel *Lady Chatterley's Lover*. Furniture, fittings and roof lead were all sold off after World War One (1914–18) and panelled rooms from the hall are housed in museums in Philadelphia and Los Angeles. Sutton Scarsdale was the home of the Leek family for many years and is a very haunted house indeed. What is left of the interior of the Hall gives rise to stories of dismembered floating arms, smells of tobacco, footsteps, and even unexplained screams. Something happened to me at Sutton Scarsdale a few years ago when I went there to take part in a BBC Radio Derby broadcast. We arrived at the front of the hall and tried to get a signal to enable us to do a live satellite link back to the radio station's base in Derby, but, just as we were about to broadcast, the signal disappeared. Thinking very quickly we instead attempted to dial the studio from a mobile phone, but again we couldn't find a signal. Undeterred, we drove around to the

other side of the building, but the same thing happened – we put up the transmitter mast but couldn't get a signal. Strangely, however, as we drove away, just 100 yards from the Hall we received a call on the mobile phone from BBC Radio Derby, asking what had happened.

The problem seems to emanate from the cellars of Sutton Scarsdale Hall; here in the bowels of the Hall are tunnels that go I do not know where. English Heritage has been renovating this fine old building and staff working here have reported smelling the stench of tobacco. Footsteps have also been heard in the inky blackness of the tunnels at Sutton Scarsdale, where it is believed some awful deed has been committed. I shudder to think what might have happened down here.

In the graveyard at Sutton Scarsdale are some of the most atmospheric and ancient gravestones I have witnessed anywhere in Derbyshire. There are legends associated with

Photo: video still.

this place. One is of Sir Francis Leek, a Royalist, who was captured by Cromwell's soldiers but escaped to join the king. As a result of his brave loyalty, he was created 1st Lord Scarsdale. When the king was executed, Sir Francis had his own grave dug at Sutton Scarsdale and every Friday he dressed in sackcloth and lay in his own open grave in commemoration of the king.

Another legend is associated with Sir Nicholas Leek, who, before he left to fight in the Crusades, took out his sword and

split his wedding ring, giving half to his wife and keeping half as a good luck token. He was captured during the Crusades and spent many years in a dark, dank prison. One day, dreaming of home, he was transported through the air and landed in the porch at the church of Sutton Scarsdale Hall. He went to the doors of his house and demanded to be let in, but he was in such a bad state that no one recognised him and he was refused entry. He then remembered that he still had his half of the split ring and he took it out of his pocket and told the servants to give it to his wife. She put the two pieces together and immediately realised her beloved had returned home. Every year after this, in thanks for his release, Sir Nicholas had bread baked for the poor people of the parish, each loaf being inscribed with a large letter 'N'. The ghost of Sir Nicholas, it is said, still haunts the porch of the church at Sutton Scarsdale Hall.

Photo: D. Redfern.

10

CHESTERFIELD

Crooked Spire

Folklore places the Devil firmly atop the major landmark in Chesterfield, which is Derbyshire's largest town. Referred to in the Domesday Book as *Cestrefeld*, meaning open field, its early prosperity was created chiefly by its role as a market town that served the whole of the north-east of Derbyshire. But this historic place has been the home of murderers, myths and legends. The last three men hanged in Derby Gaol all hailed from Chesterfield. On 10 August 1888, Arthur Thomas Delaney was executed for the murder of his wife at Chesterfield; on 30 July 1902, John Bedford was hanged for the murder of Nancy Price at Duckmanton; and on 29 December 1905, John Silk went the same way for the murder of his mother at Chesterfield. The town, which claims stronger links with the south Yorkshire city of Sheffield than the county city of Derby, is surrounded by some of the most beautiful unspoilt countryside in the county. Built over a Roman site, it is also situated on top of an Iron Age fort. The Romans probably settled here because the area is so rich in natural minerals like coal, lead and tin.

The famous crooked spire at St Mary's and All Saints Parish Church dominates the skyline for miles around. It is said to have twisted many years ago through a combination of heavy lead cladding and unseasoned timbers used in its construction. However, I much prefer the story that claims the Devil landed on the church one day, twisting his tail

around the spire to secure him as he looked down on the town. A wedding was taking place and as the newly-weds emerged from the parish church, the Devil noticed the bride was wearing white. In shock and horror the Devil flew down to look at the bride and groom, forgetting to unravel his tail from the spire. It twisted as a result. So what was the reason for the Devil's urgency? Folklore states the bride was a virgin – and the Devil had never seen a virgin bride in Chesterfield before!

The Theatre Ghosts

Across the road from the Parish Church of St Mary's and All Saints in Corporation Street is the town's theatre. Formerly known as The Civic, the 500-seat theatre is now called The Pomegranate and staff here have reported poltergeist activity and ghost sightings. Objects are said to move around for no reason and there have been sightings too of an old lady with

Photo: S. Lilley.

grey hair, wearing a grey dress apparently in mourning for her husband. Famous English engineer George Stephenson, who built the first steam locomotive engine, was born in 1781 and died in Chesterfield in 1848. He is said to haunt the stage of the Pomegranate Theatre and has been seen striding proudly across the stage. Theatre directors sitting alone in the balcony area, pondering over changes to a forthcoming production, have seen doors to the balcony open and close. Regular visitors to the Pomegranate now greet these interruptions with the words: 'Oh, is that you George?' Stephenson actually died at Tapton House, a fine Georgian mansion near Chesterfield that he bought 10 years before his death.

Exorcism in New Square, Chesterfield

In Chesterfield's New Square is a haunted house that once belonged to a Doctor Jones. A branch of the Yorkshire Bank

Photo: S. Lilley.

has now been built on this site, but in bygone days when Doctor Jones owned the property he rather confusingly called his home the Old Manor House, which it was not. There are various ghost stories connected with this building. A lady who once lived there told the story of an aunt, visiting for the day, who saw on the top floor of the building a little girl wandering along the corridor. Surprised and wondering what the girl was doing there, she bent down to pick up the child, but her hands and arms passed straight through the apparition. In her fright, this woman flew down the stairs without touching any of them! The same lady's grandmother had also seen the ghost of a man wandering around the dining room shackled by chains. She could hear the clanking of the chains and, terrified, she slammed the dining room door shut and locked it, waiting outside on the pavement for her husband's return. Breathing fast and relieved that she was now safe, her relative calm turned to wild panic again when she heard the clanking of the chains coming through the door! At this, she probably picked up her skirt and hot-

Photo: S. Lilley.

footed it through the streets of Chesterfield. Another member of the family saw something so horrific in this same house that she couldn't bear to tell anyone what she had witnessed. However, though petrified, she solved the situation herself by performing her own form of exorcism. She threw the Holy Bible at the fearsome ghost, and it was never seen again.

The Chesterfield burglar who returned in death

In 1675 a rather intriguing pamphlet was circulated in the streets of London. It told of strange happenings in Chesterfield. A section of the pamphlet read:

> *Strange and terrible news from Chesterfield in Derbyshire! Being a full and true relation of a horrible and terrible ghost that was visibly seen on Sunday 24th January 1674, first in the shape of a dog, then a woman, and afterwards a man, together with the discovery of some money that was hidden by him in his lifetime as a burglar.*

The pamphlet was signed by Richard Hobbs, constable, James Nitt, constable, Joseph Wilson, churchwarden, and Mr Brown, gentleman and it relates to an interesting and spooky incident of an old couple that, in 1674, spent a series of restless nights being disturbed by three apparitions. On the first night, they awoke to hear a loud banging on the door at half-past three in the morning. The old man went downstairs and opened the door to find a large black dog, growling and snarling at him. In alarm, he slammed the door shut and went back to bed. The next night the same banging awoke the old couple again and, bravely, the man lit a candle and once more descended the staircase and opened the door, this time to discover a woman draped in white clothing that was stained

Photo: video still.

with the vivid red of blood. Again he slammed the door shut and returned to bed. On the third night, the hammering on the door was heard for a third time and the old man again plucked up the courage to descend the staircase and open the heavy door. This time he saw a man standing wearing black clothes. Though his first instinct was again to slam the door in the face of another impostor, the old man was fascinated by this larger than life figure with his soft, persuasive voice. Won over, the old man agreed to follow the spectre as it made its way to a nearby field. Here, the old man was told, was lost treasure, the spectre's ill-gotten booty buried for safekeeping from burglaries he had committed in life. The treasure was uncovered and the figure in black asked the old man to return it to its rightful owners. The old man scrupulously followed the spectre's time-consuming wishes, and legend has it that the figure in black – its conscience now salved – was never seen again.

II

THE BULL I'TH THORN

The main road between Ashbourne and Buxton in the northern reaches of Derbyshire can be a bleak place and here is to be found reputedly the oldest inn in county. A dwelling has been on this site since 1472 – before the Battle of Bosworth – and it has been an inn since the 1660s. Such a place of remote antiquity must have its fair share of ghosts, and the landlady has many paranormal experiences to recount to locals and casual visitors alike. I can certainly confirm, from personal experience, that the Bull i'th Thorn has one of the creakiest front doors I have ever encountered – and this sets the tone of this haunted inn. Bull i'th Thorn actually means 'Bull in a thorn bush' and it has long been a favourite place of mine. I used to take in people on haunted Derbyshire coach tours many years ago and the Bull i'th

Photo: S. Lilley.

Thorn was always a great place to stop off for liquid refreshment combined with a good ghost story! In those days the current landlady, Annette, worked behind the bar and her association with this ancient inn is far more intimate than mine. She believes that several ghosts probably haunt this place, but all seem quite happy to be there. Several bed and breakfast guests have experienced items falling off walls, including mirrors, and some have even felt the strange sensation of having their hair touched when apparently no other living person was in the same room.

Annette regularly senses that she is not alone in the pub – even when she actually is – and though she says she has never physically seen a ghost in the Bull i'th Thorn, others most definitely have. No one is quite sure who the ghosts are, but one, who sits on a little box in the pub, is known as 'Little Jenny'. At one time a medium was invited in and made contact with this girl, claiming she was someone who died during the Great Plague in the 1600s. Her parents apparently died while she was still small, which is why Little Jenny sits there waiting for them to return. Annette says Jenny can be a naughty little girl because she pinches things. Pub staff report having put items such as knives and forks down on a table only for them to disappear, reappearing somewhere else. Annette has taken to admonishing this cheeky spirit with the words: 'Look Jenny, put it back!' She also tells Jenny not to frighten the pub's customers, especially children.

The Bull i'th Thorn also boasts a dead man's chair. Apparently the chair came from Chatsworth House and belonged to William Cavendish, Earl of Devonshire. It was moved out of the Derbyshire stately home, along with other pieces of furniture, after a fire and for some reason – no one knows why – it appeared at this inn. Now cordoned off in an

attempt to preserve it, the chair is said to be a favourite resting place of the ghost of an old man.

These tales add to the special atmosphere of the Bull i'th Thorn. In my experiences of this pub, I have always sensed that *something* is going on here. As with so many other hauntings, I can offer nothing more tangible than the power of my own senses, but I defy anyone to sit alone in the bar of this ancient public house at dead of night and not feel altogether uncomfortable.

II
ARBOR LOW: DERBYSHIRE'S STONEHENGE

Arbor Low is Derbyshire's Stonehenge. In the care of English Heritage, it is situated in the middle of the county on a high point 375 metres above sea level. It is magical and the stones have been in place for well over 3,000 years. In fact it is the finest Stone Age 'henge' monument in the north of England and is designated now as a site of unique archaeological and cultural interest. Although the view from Arbor Low on a fine day is stunning, it can be a bleak place in bad weather and you would be brave indeed to venture there at night.

Constructed in about 2500 BC, no one knows why it was built or what it was used for, but clearly it was a focal point for the people of the time. It comprises a circular bank, 76 metres in diameter by two metres high, with inside it a ditch about 1.5 metres deep enclosing a circular central sanctuary

area. Entrances can be found at the north-west and south-east of the bank. There are 59 stones in total, of different sizes, all now lying flat. No one knows if originally the stones stood upright, but it is thought early Christians may have lain them flat in order to 'de-sanctify' the site. However there is no archaeological evidence to support this. In any event, the stones may well have been added after the construction of the original henge, which probably featured wooden posts in the early years.

Adding to Arbor Low's haunted status is the fact that several burials were excavated there in 1845 by Thomas Bateman. Nearby lies Gib Hill, a Bronze Age burial mound. As long as there has been life there have been stories of death and this is one of the reasons why Arbor Low is such a special place. Ancient Britons going back at least 5,000 years believed in an after-life that went on under the ground. They believed when someone died the soul passed on from one person to another and when the Romans invaded they couldn't understand why these people were such ferocious fighters – it was because they believed death wasn't the end and that they went on to an afterlife.

The huge stones, now lying down at Arbor Low, look like a clock face. I believe in stone tapes – the theory that stones are able to hold a story just like videotapes and cassette tapes. I believe stone can hold a recording when tragic traumatic premature death happens, as in accidents and sacrifices. The number of human sacrifices that must have gone on here is a reason for it being so haunted. People who live nearby will still not venture onto this site at night for fear of boggarts. Many years ago I was reading a book about dousing in which the author related that many years ago he went to Aylesbury and touched the stones. He felt the energy

move through his hand, through his body and to a crystal that began to move of its own accord. Touching the stones at Arbor Low is similar – like plugging into a 13-amp socket. When I tried the experiment with the crystal, although I couldn't actually feel the energy coming through, the crystal moved without my moving my hand at all. When I pulled my hand away it was like unplugging. This sort of experience proves to me that there is more to heaven and earth than any of us realise.

13

THE NINE LADIES
STONE CIRCLE

Derbyshire is very much a place of legend and mystery, of stone circles and burial grounds. Most tend to be in the northern Dark Peak regions, but Stanton Moor is more centrally located not far from the town of Matlock. Druids, witches, hikers and others who are just plain curious regularly make their way to this fascinatingly remote place situated near the high-ground settlements of Birchover, Stanton in Peak and Stanton Lees. The Nine Ladies can be a strange and forbidding place, and it dates back to the Bronze Age. There have been many burials here and many a haunting too. The visitor leaves all signs of civilisation behind at Stanton Moor and it is definitely not a place where you would want to lose your way as dusk turns quickly to night. The spectre of a large black dog has been seen wandering the hills in these parts, darting in and out of the shadows of trees. A man dressed in

Photo: video still.

black has often been seen too, standing on the outer perimeter of the stones, while a lady in grey has been seen walking the lonely pathways around this remote area.

Then of course there is the special legend attached to the stone circle itself. Why is it known as the Nine Ladies? It is said that Stanton Moor is where nine ladies danced daringly on the Sabbath. On a large stone, known as the 'Fiddler's Chair', sat the Devil himself, playing the fiddle for the ladies to dance. God was not happy at this and turned the nine ladies into stone – and there they have remained, still to be seen to this day. Is Stanton Moor then Derbyshire's own Sodom and Gomorrah?

Then the Lord rained upon Sodom and upon Gomorrah brimstone and fire from the Lord out of heaven; And he overthrew those cities, and all the plain, and all the inhabitants of the cities, and that which grew upon the ground. But his [Lot's] wife looked back from behind him, and she became a pillar of salt.

– Genesis 19: 24–26 (King James Version)

14

TISSINGTON HALL

Derbyshire can boast a host of imposing stately homes, so it's only natural that these fine houses, steeped in history, should be at the centre of tales of hauntings. One such place is Tissington Hall, the focal point of possibly one of the most beautiful and unspoiled villages in the whole of the county. Famed for its well dressings and picture postcard estate cottages, Tissington can be traced back as far as 1086, when it is mentioned as Tizinctun in the Domesday Book. This name probably derives from Old English or Anglo-Saxon, meaning Tidsige's Farm. In 1259, the Tissington estate passed to the Meynell family and then to the FitzHerberts,

Photo: S. Lilley.

who have held it for the best part of 500 years, and over this time, a fascinating collection of historical records has been built up about the area and the family.

Tissington is listed in the Domesday Book among the possessions of Henry de Ferrers. The estate passed to the Savage family in the time of Henry I and William le Savage, the last male heir, died in 1259. Two co-heiresses of Savage then bought the manor for the families of Meynell and Edensor. In the Meynell family, the estate passed down the generations to Joan Meynell, who carried it to her second husband, Sir Thomas Clynton, whose only daughter and heiress, Anne, married Robert Franceys of Foremark. Again there was an only daughter, Cicely, who inherited the estate and who married Nicholas FitzHerbert of Somersall. Thus it was that half of the manor of Tissington came into the FitzHerbert family through a chain of heiresses of Savage, Meynell, Clynton and Franceys.

In the reign of Elizabeth I, Francis FitzHerbert, the great-grandson of Nicholas, purchased it and so the Manor of Tissington was again under the ownership of a single family.

Since that time, the history of this pretty Derbyshire village has been inextricably linked to that of the FitzHerbert family, who still occupy the Hall and run an estate extending from Bradbourne Mill in the east, to the River Dove in the west.

The present incumbent, Sir Richard FitzHerbert, has his own ghost story. He showed me a gallery landing on the top floor of the Hall and immediately I could sense that the atmosphere was slightly strange. This gallery has guest bedrooms leading off and Sir Richard knows that a gentlewoman in days gone by met her death in one particular room. Apparently a fire broke out in the night, caused when

candles set alight heavy curtains. The unfortunate woman was soon alight herself and tried in vain to wrap herself in her bed covers to put out the inferno. By this time, however, the bedclothes too were blazing and it was only through the intervention of her sister that the fire was eventually put out. The woman, however, was so badly burned that she died several weeks later from her injuries after being treated unsuccessfully by various local apothecaries. Sir Richard told me there was a suspicion that one of these concoctions was administered in error and may have hastened her death.

Although folklore has it that the ghost of the woman still haunts the top floor of Tissington Hall, it took a piece of modern-day technology to reignite the legend. Sir Richard

hired in engineers to carry out a condition survey of the roof and video footage was filmed as part of the project. It was a simple exercise that involved no fancy special effects, but on playing back the video the engineer was genuinely shaken up by what he saw on the section of film that was shot in the actual bedroom where the woman died. On it was the image of a half-length portrait falling onto the floor. However, there was no painting whatsoever in the room at the time.

Other visitors to the Hall have seen images of a young girl on the landing. Sir Richard himself hasn't actually seen the woman who burned to death or the little girl, but says he has caught sight of images around the house that he believes are of a benevolent nature. From my visit to this historic place, I am sure certain energies from the past remain in the house, and indeed the local vicar has been called in to bless the haunted bedroom. Sir Richard must have a strong constitution because apparently, apart from one woman in the village, he is the only person living who has had the nerve to sleep alone in Tissington Hall.

FURTHER RESEARCH

If you have been caught by the ghost-hunting bug after reading about our adventures in Derbyshire, the following publications and DVDs may be of interest to you.

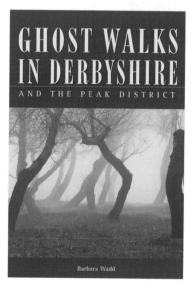
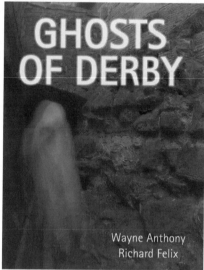

Books:

Richard Felix and Wayne Anthony *Ghosts of Derby*, Breedon Books, reprinted 2005.

Barbara Wadd *Ghost Walks in Derbyshire and the Peak District*, Breedon Books, reprinted 2005.

Both of the above books are available from all good bookshops and may also be purchased at the Heritage Centre in Derby or direct from the publishers, Breedon Books, 3 The Parker Centre, Mansfield Road, Derby, DE21 4SZ, tel 01332 384 325, fax 01332 292 755, email sales@breedonpublishing.co.uk.

DVDs:

Derby Ghosts with *Most Haunted*'s Richard Felix
The Most Haunted Places In Derby with *Most Haunted*'s Richard Felix
Derbyshire Ghosts 2 with *Most Haunted*'s Richard Felix

All these DVDs, as well as many others from the Ghost Tour of Great Britain, are available from shops in Derby, the Heritage Centre, and direct from the producers, Film Studios Ltd, 35 Eaton Bank, Duffield, Derby, DE56 4BJ, tel 01332 840 292. Order online at www.ghostdvds.co.uk

INDEX